T0326364

The Last Laugh

German Film Classics

Also in the series:

THE LAST LAUGH

SAMUEL FREDERICK

 CAMDEN HOUSE

First published 2023 by Camden House

Camden House is an imprint of Boydell & Brewer Inc.
668 Mt. Hope Avenue, Rochester, NY 14620, USA
and of Boydell & Brewer Limited
PO Box 9, Woodbridge, Suffolk IP12 3DF, UK
www.boydellandbrewer.com

Cover image: The porter (Emil Jannings) emerges
from the revolving door in a dream image from
The Last Laugh. Screenshot.

ISBN-13: 978-1-64014-129-2

Library of Congress Cataloging-in-Publication Data

CIP data is available from the Library of Congress.

This publication is printed on acid-free paper.
Printed in the United States of America.

Publication of this book was supported by a grant from the
German Film Institute (GFI) of the University of Michigan
Department of Germanic Languages & Literatures.

In memory of David Bathrick (1936–2020)

CONTENTS

ACKNOWLEDGMENTS

I am grateful to a number of colleagues and friends for help on this book. Sabine Doran provided last-minute insight on one detail that was essential. Cameron Bushnell helped me with some rhetorical finesse. Janet Bergstrom graciously responded to my email queries about Murnau. Megan Wadas helpfully translated selections from Pier Giorgio Tone's Murnau book. Jens Guettel helped me with the historical context and suggested key sources. Hannah Matangos shared some incisive views on the film that got me through a tricky part of the revisions. David Rando read the whole manuscript for redundancies and infelicities. Jon Abel provided excellent suggestions and critiques on the manuscript that made it a better book.

Production stills were provided by the Deutsche Kinemathek in Berlin. The lithograph by Theo Matejko and the production sketch by Robert Herlth and Walter Röhrig were provided by the Cinémathèque française in Paris. The latter sketch is reproduced with the kind permission of Andreas, Alexander, and Nikolai Luckow (the grandsons of Robert Herlth).

The College of Liberal Arts at Penn State generously gave me funds for a research trip and to pay for the images. I thank Carrie Jackson, Interim Head of the Department of Germanic and Slavic Languages and Literatures, for appealing on my behalf.

Special thanks go to Brad Prager, who took my ideas to Camden House in the first place, to the series editors Gerd Gemünden and Johannes von Moltke for their support and feedback, and lastly but most importantly to Jim Walker for his incredible enthusiasm and support at every stage.

The Last Laugh

In an audacious downward movement, the opening shot of Friedrich Wilhelm Murnau's 1924 feature *Der letzte Mann*, known in English as *The Last Laugh*, plunges the viewer into a dynamic urban scene. As the light first illuminates the screen, we find ourselves already in motion, inside an elevator that is descending from on high into a hotel lobby below. The open construction of the cage-style lift affords a wide view, which the subjective camera captures in deep focus and with a slight high-angled tilt, making a long stretch of the vestibule visible as it approaches, abustle with guests coming and going.

This descent inaugurated a completely new era in cinema. Contemporary viewers were not shy about announcing the sea change. In his review of the film, Willy Haas called it revolutionary: "Well, kids, from here on out begins a new epoch in the history of cinematics [*Kinematographie*]!"[1] The magazine *Die Filmwoche* declared *The Last Laugh*'s premiere "the true birth of film as a form of art," claiming that "everything that happened before was only a step on the way to this accomplishment."[2] For indeed, before *The Last Laugh*, the camera was almost always static, chained as it was to the immobile tripod. With some exceptions, which I will discuss later in the book, the moving images created in cinema's first three decades had to be contained within a stubbornly unmoving frame. With Murnau's film the camera is fully "unchained": the frame that had hitherto limited access to the space around it is now able to roam about freely in all directions. This technical innovation transforms the camera's capacities to capture the world in all its protean flux by participating in that very flux. The consequences of this newfound mobility cannot be overstated. Film critic Andrew Sarris goes so far as to say that because of the mobile camera, "Murnau's influence on the cinema has proved to be more lasting than Eisenstein's." The reason for this enduring impact, for Sarris, comes down to Murnau's realism. The moving camera, he writes, provides "a more suitable style for exploring the world than does Eisenstein's dialectical montage, and the trend in modern movies has been toward escaping studio sets so as to discover the real world."[3]

Although it may escape the ballast of the tripod, *The Last Laugh* never leaves the set. Shot on Ufa Studios backlots in Berlin-Tempelhof and Potsdam-Babelsberg (what is today Babelsberg Studio), the real world it offers to viewers is an elaborate illusion. And yet, this film comes closer than any of Murnau's preceding works to presenting contemporary German life soberly and candidly.[4] 1924 was a turning point for Murnau, as for Germany as a whole, which for the first time since before the war experienced something resembling normalcy. The preceding decade had been a tumultuous time of uncertainty, from war to (failed) revolutions to stifling hyperinflation. A film about the fickle turns of fate, *The Last Laugh* obliquely alludes to these recent crises and to the transition from stability to calamity—and possibly back again. It is a film about change: both unexpected and unwanted transformations as well as astonishing and fortuitous ones. It explores the precariousness of modern urban life with honesty and compassion.

This book will provide an in-depth contextualization and analysis of *The Last Laugh*, placing special emphasis on its technical and formal innovations and on its position at a transitional moment in the socioeconomic history of Germany. This historical juncture happens also to align with a critical shift in the aesthetic practices of German cinema away from Expressionism and towards a more unassuming realism. Surveying these changes in the film industry will help identify Murnau's particular contributions to cinematic language, which I will explore in detailed analyses of key scenes, paying close attention to the mise-en-scène (especially the role of lighting, objects, and framing) and to the cinematographic activation of space (especially as made possible by the newly "unchained" camera). This formal analysis will in turn dovetail with a thorough investigation of the film's thematic concerns, which are never far removed from the sociopolitical realities of the Weimar period, all with the goal of painting a detailed picture of a film that forever changed what moving pictures could accomplish.

Today, F. W. Murnau's name is synonymous with the golden age of Weimar silent cinema. In 1952, a little over two decades after his untimely death, film historian Lotte Eisner declared Murnau "the greatest film-director the Germans have ever known."[5] Many scholars, filmmakers, and cinephiles still agree with this assessment.[6] Murnau began making films in 1919, after having acted in Max Reinhardt's theater troupe and having served as a fighter pilot in the war. His early films, highly atmospheric and often fantastical, made use of the forms and tropes of cinematic Expressionism, which he stamped with his own distinctive style. He combined richly layered and meticulous lighting with masterly framing, bringing what Thomas Elsaesser calls a "painterly eye and pictorial sensibility" together with "high-tech perfectionism" to create otherworldly spaces at the indeterminate border between dream and reality.[7] These are spaces saturated in an inimitable mood, concocted with equal parts melancholy, eroticism, and enigma. Murnau's (closeted) homosexuality no doubt inflected the idiosyncratic gaze that takes in these spaces, a gaze that captures figures of passion with ambivalent longing, at times privileging objects and architecture over human forms.[8] These films enact a desire that lies in looking itself, an intrinsically cinematic devotion to the vicissitudes of light and shadow that constitute our world. Murnau pursued this devotion assiduously, developing his "unparalleled poetry of the image" in the fourteen feature films he directed prior to *The Last Laugh*.[9] Although many of these pictures were greeted with great acclaim, it was his 1922 adaptation of Bram Stoker's *Dracula*, whose titular vampire was renamed Nosferatu to avoid copyright infringement, that catapulted Murnau to international prominence as one of Germany's finest directors.[10]

Like his contemporaries Ernst Lubitsch and Fritz Lang, as well as a slightly younger generation including Billy Wilder and Edgar G. Ulmer, the latter of whom worked as a set design assistant on *The Last Laugh*, Murnau ended up in Hollywood.[11] According to set designer Robert Herlth, it was the technical innovations of *The Last Laugh* that were responsible for Fox Studios inviting Murnau to come to Southern California. "There was a telegram from Hollywood addressed to Ufa, asking what camera we had used to shoot the film," Herlth recalls. "It added that in the USA there was no such camera, and no town to compare with the one in our film."[12] Murnau made two more pictures for Ufa—*Tartuffe* (1925) and *Faust* (1926), in both of which, as in *The Last Laugh*, Emil Jannings played a leading role— before departing for Hollywood. There he made four features, the first of which, *Sunrise* (1927), won three Oscars, including for "Best Unique and Artistic Picture," at the first Academy Awards in 1929.[13] At the same ceremony, "Best Actor" went to Jannings for his role in Josef von Sternberg's *The Last Command*, further demonstrating how important German talent was in Hollywood at the time. Although Murnau lived to see the transition from silent film to sound, he did not live long enough to make a talkie.[14] His final film, *Tabu: A Story of the South Seas*, a stunning docufictional feature shot together with Robert Flaherty on the South Pacific island of Bora Bora, premiered on March 19, 1931, exactly one week after Murnau died in a hospital in Santa Barbara after suffering serious injuries in a car accident the day before. He was forty-two.

The First Title Cards and the Last Man

The Last Laugh starts with a sparse opening credit title card on which we find only the name of the film above the names of Emil Jannings ("In the Lead Role") and F. W. Murnau ("Direction"), in that order. Credits for script, scenery, camera, and supporting roles have been omitted, part of the film's general tendency to suppress non-diegetic text and thereby create the effect of an uninterrupted sequence of images. For aside from these truncated opening credits, *The Last Laugh* includes only two title cards. The first of these comes immediately after these opening credits; that is, even before the first shot of the film: "Today you are the first, respected by everyone, a minister, a general, maybe even a prince—Do you know what you'll be tomorrow?!" Both because it does not interrupt the film's images and also because it does not introduce the setting, characters, or action of the story that follows, this first title card does not really function as a proper "inter"-title. Instead, it presents a thematic epigraph that belongs with the non-diegetic metadiscourse of the opening credits.[15]

The status of the second title card (and only proper intertitle of the film), the text of which we will look at closely later in the book, while it does come between the film's images, is similarly complicated by its metadiscursive content. Moreover, as we will see, this sole intertitle functions more as a hard break than a temporary interruption, introducing what is best taken as an alternative ending rather than the continuation of the story. In this way, *The Last Laugh*'s two title cards function as bookends to the main story it tells, carefully placed to maximize the sense that the entire picture unfolds fluidly, without the interruptions that convey dialogue and identify characters or key occurrences, which were customary for any feature-length production (as well as most shorts) of the silent period. Even the standard division of the film into acts—it was scripted with six—is not indicated in any way. Only a small amount of diegetic text (in the forms of a letter, writing on a cake, and a newspaper article) helps provide key information without having to resort to title cards, which would have required cuts away from the action and back. Without these insertions, *The Last Laugh* achieves a sustained focus on its subject-matter using strictly visual means, its uninterrupted flow of images creating the illusion of seamless temporal movement, a movement complemented and intensified, as we will see, by the film's revolutionary mobile camera.

The Last Laugh was not the first feature-length film to forego intertitles. Murnau was following a short-lived trend begun by his screenwriter Carl Mayer, whose scripts for *Hintertreppe* (Backstairs, 1921), directed by Leopold Jessner with Paul Leni, and two Lupu Pick features, *Scherben* (Shattered, 1921) and *Sylvester* (New Year's Eve, 1924), all excluded titles and minimized diegetic text. Coming between these last two films, Artur Robison's *Schatten* (Warning Shadows, 1923) was also titleless. Nevertheless, despite not being the very first, and despite not even being *entirely* without title cards, *The Last Laugh* remains the most famous of these early experiments in eliminating the usual textual interruptions between images. It certainly received the credit for this innovation—deserved or not.[16] As a reporter at the American premiere wrote, "For me and likely also for most other Americans the lack of titles alone was a sensation in itself."[17] Decades later, in his interviews with François Truffaut, Alfred Hitchcock said of his attempt to minimize titles in his early film *The Farmer's Wife* (1928), that "the only film made without any titles at all was *The Last Laugh*."[18] To his biographer Donald Spoto, Hitchcock elaborated: "*The Last Laugh* was almost the perfect film. It told its story even without subtitles [*sic*]—from beginning to end entirely by the use of imagery, and that had a tremendous influence on me."[19] The excitement about the possibility of creating a titleless film went well beyond Europe and the United States. *The Last Laugh* premiered in early 1926 in Japan, resulting in a long debate on its camerawork and lack of titles in the pages of the film journal *Eiga orai*. In a poll later that year, director Teinosuke Kinugasa named Murnau's picture his favorite film ever, saying he had watched it five times. Kinugasa's early masterpiece *Kurutta ippeiji* (A Page of Madness, 1926), which began production soon after *The Last Laugh*'s Tokyo premiere, is completely without title cards.[20] It is a testament

Figure 1. Advertisement for *The Last Laugh* in the Japanese newspaper *Asahi shinbun*, March 26, 1926 (evening edition), here called a "controversial" film with "no titles." Special thanks to Jonathan E. Abel for alerting me to this ad and for translating it.

to its association with this innovation (and to the exclusion of the few other films that had done it first), that *The Last Laugh* was advertised in Germany, the United States, and Japan as having been the first film to attain the artistic achievement of eschewing intertitles.[21] And yet, perhaps because of its underperformance at the box office, Ufa later distributed a version of the film with intertitles added, clearly against Mayer and Murnau's wishes.[22]

What are we to make of the epigraph to this film that otherwise contains so little further text? "Today you are the first, respected by everyone, a minister, a general, maybe even a prince—Do you know what you'll be tomorrow?!" Instead of situating us in time and space, or introducing our protagonist, this first title card sets up the story that follows with an ethically-charged question, inviting the viewer to identify with its titular character. The allusion to this figure and his fate comes, before we even see him on the screen, from the juxtaposition of the title, *Der letzte Mann*, "The Last Man," prominently displayed in the opening credits, with the epigraph's subsequent reference to being among "the first." This contrast suggests that being "the last" is what becomes of those who are—indeed, are recognized by "everyone" else as—"the first." The sentiment may echo the words of Jesus ("the first shall be last," Matthew 20:16), though here it has been transposed into the secular and political realm of government, military, and even monarchy.

And yet the fall of a great man is not really the story of *The Last Laugh*. Emil Jannings plays an elderly head porter at the classy Atlantic hotel in an unnamed big city. He may have the look and demeanor of an important man, donning a stately uniform that recalls the general of the epigraph and with a prominent moustache that suggests the emperor-regent Wilhelm II (who had abdicated in 1918), but he calls a lower-class tenement his home. As the film starts, we see him hard at work in front of the hotel, protecting guests from the rain with his umbrella as he helps them into taxis. He takes pride in his work, which he initially appears to carry out with poise and confidence. But soon some guests arrive with a large travel chest, which the porter—after using his whistle in vain to call for help—is only barely able to carry into the hotel by himself. Exhausted by this exertion, he briefly sits down in the lobby to rest and have a drink of water. The manager sees him there, noting his apparent frailty. As the porter returns to his post, the rain ceases. Removing his oilskin coat to reveal a splendorous uniform, he briefly glances in a pocket mirror to make sure his hair and mustache are presentable, then continues saluting guests and helping them into taxis.

The next scene shows the porter returning to the tenement apartments where he lives with his daughter.[23] He wears his uniform home and his neighbors greet him with kindness and respect. We learn that the porter's daughter is about to marry. We see her the next morning preparing her wedding cake, as her father, in front of the mirror, gets ready for work. But when he arrives at the hotel, entering the lobby through the central revolving door, he is shocked to find a younger uniformed man making his way to his post. In the next scene, the manager gives our protagonist a letter explaining that due to his age and frailty he is being demoted to washroom attendant. Devastated, the porter tries to demonstrate his strength to the manager by lifting a large trunk, but falls down under its weight.

His uniform is subsequently removed from him and locked away in a closet, but the demoted porter manages to pocket the key. With a plain white washroom smock and a stack of towels in hand, he is sent downstairs to work at his new post.

In the evening, we see that the wedding celebration is already underway as the old man gets off work. Eluding the flashlight of the night watchman, he sneaks into the manager's office and takes the uniform. Wearing it, he arrives at the party, where we meet the groom and the groom's aunt, who, along with the rest of the guests, enthusiastically welcome the bride's father. At the party's end, after the guests have dispersed, the old man stumbles about drunkenly before falling asleep in a chair. Here he dreams that he is a fantastically powerful porter who impresses everyone at the hotel by easily lifting a heavy trunk and even tossing it into the air. Upon waking, the groom's aunt helps him into his uniform and lovingly sends him off to work, where, seeing the new head porter, he is reminded of his downfall. Storing the uniform at the train station, he returns to the hotel's underground washroom, where we see him sleepily at work. The aunt, however, has planned a surprise visit with a homecooked lunch. When she finds the old man not at his post in front of the revolving door but in the subterranean washroom, she returns in horror to the tenement to tell her nephew's new wife. An eavesdropping neighbor overhears her revelation and the news swiftly spreads throughout the tenement, so that when the ex-porter returns home wearing his uniform at the end of the day, he is beset with mocking laughter. In a subsequent scene, his daughter, her husband, and his aunt appear to banish him.

The ex-porter returns to the hotel holding—not wearing—his uniform, which he gives to the night watchman, who returns it to the manager's office while the dejected old man heads down to the washroom. There, the night watchman places a coat over him and the film fades to black. At this point we get the only proper intertitle of the film, which informs us that in the epilogue to follow, "the author" has taken pity on our protagonist, giving his story a happy, if unlikely, ending. In this epilogue we learn that by pure chance the old man inherited a fortune from a multimillionaire who died in the washroom. As the story of the ex-porter's luck spreads through the hotel, we find him in the restaurant indulging in a grotesquely expansive feast. The night watchman, his only friend, soon joins him. The film ends with the two departing from the hotel by horse-drawn carriage, waving to the staff assembled in front of the revolving door.

If at the start of *The Last Laugh* we meet a man who straddles the worlds of the first and the last, Murnau goes on to show us what happens when this balancing act fails: demotion in one world leads to dishonor in the other and to expulsion from both. Underlying this banishment is the dark truth that the porter never really was "the first" in either realm. Ultimately, the trajectory of his decline appears to be from "first" not just to "last" (lowest in rank or standing) but to "final" (a decisive and irrevocable end). Given this picture of downfall and degradation, is the response of empathy Murnau invites us to have sufficient? Is it proper? Does Murnau's own model of such a response in the contrived epilogue shame us for failing to respond or does it make fun of our inability to accept the fate we are all dealt? Either way, *The Last Laugh* leaves us with little to laugh about, whether we are among "the first" or have suffered with "the last."

Germany at a Crossroads

To begin to answer these questions, we need to look at the film's historical context, for the decline that the film represents in the fate of an individual can only be properly understood against the backdrop of the collective experience of the young German state, what we now call the Weimar Republic, which had just emerged from several years of crisis following the end of the First World War. Indeed, the date of *The Last Laugh*'s production and release, 1924, was the first year since the war in which Germany achieved something like political and economic stability. As historian Detlev Peukert puts it, the "degree of calm that arrived in 1924 ... is very striking" compared to the struggles of 1920–1923, which were "among the most hectic and eventful of the Weimar Republic." In some ways, Peukert maintains, "the world war of 1914–1918 did not end until 1923."[24]

Germany did not only lose the war; it had to accept responsibility for "all the loss and damage" the Allies suffered. This was the language of the Treaty of Versailles, signed in 1919 and implemented at the start of 1920, which also stipulated Germany's disarmament, territorial concessions, and reparations. The latter became a source of intensifying socioeconomic uncertainty in the immediate postwar years, in part because Germany was left without a fixed amount of reparations, which would only be settled on in 1921 (at 269 billion gold marks) and then revised soon after (to 132 billion).[25] Although the financial burden of these reparations was considerable for the young republic, in many ways its impact was less economic than social and cultural. For the average German, the demand for reparations heaped insult upon the still sore injury of the defeat, leading to anxieties and humiliation that in some spheres festered into outright resentment, all of which spilled over into everyday life.

At the same time, political unrest seemed to be escalating. There was an attempted, but failed, coup in March 1920 led by Wolfgang Kapp and Walther von Lüttwitz, who wanted to overturn the newly established democratic government and impose an autocratic regime. Because there was no strong military response to the Kapp putsch (indeed, those Reichswehr members who did not join the coup nonetheless refused to take up arms against it), the labor unions organized a general strike, supported by the Social Democrats and the communists. Another left-wing workers' uprising in the Ruhr area only weeks later resulted in over one thousand deaths. Social and political uncertainty persisted for years, punctuated by violence and turmoil, including the assassinations of former finance minister Mathias Erzberger in August 1921 and foreign minister Walther

Rathenau in June 1922, as well as the attempted assassination of former minister-president Philipp Scheidemann, just twenty days before Rathenau's murder. The ultra-nationalist group Organisation Consul were behind all three attacks.

These crises came to a head in 1923 on two fronts: international politics and the domestic economy. When Germany defaulted on its reparation payments in early January, France and Belgium occupied the Ruhr region. The occupation resulted in a widespread campaign of passive resistance and civil disobedience, which had to be financed. The already frail economy and rising inflation then took a dramatic turn for the worse, leading to a total collapse of the German currency. Peukert paints a dire picture in numbers: "In January 1923 the wholesale price index was already 2,783 times higher than its 1913 level; by December 1923 it was 1,261 thousand million [i.e., billion] times higher." The paper mark effectively "lost its function as a medium of payment."[26] Indeed, on November 2, 1923 the Reichsbank issued a 100-trillion-mark note, and by the end of the month the exchange rate was $1 = 4.2 trillion marks.[27] These circumstances led to a drastic decline in living standards, to a sharp increase in unemployment, to food shortages, and to strikes. As historian Eric D. Weitz writes, the "overall effect" was "a severe disruption of the boundaries between social groups."[28]

Peukert points to these dual crises as precipitating a national reassessment: "Germans were brought to accept the true scale of their defeat abroad and of economic distress at home, after having refused to face up to these facts in the years since 1918." Ultimately, "1923 was a nadir" and it "left a profound imprint on the German psyche."[29] That same November saw Hitler's Munich Beer Hall putsch, which catapulted the future dictator into the center of attention. Weitz articulates this period of national desperation and social resentment in terms of a self-destructive blame-game that heightened disorder and strife among all social levels: "In Germany in 1923, there was precious little empathy for others."[30] The relative calm of 1924 ushered in by currency reform and the Dawes Plan (which included a staggered repayment plan for reparations and a $200 million loan from the United States) allowed for a rare moment of reflection and a critical scrutiny of the immediate past. This was a much-needed moment of self-examination, one in which Murnau's film from this year, too, participated.

Indeed, *The Last Laugh* dramatizes the contradictions of this period with complexity and nuance. It presents a figure who appears to embody the old world working on the threshold of the new, someone whose downfall and humiliation makes palpable a rift not previously evident. The empathy that Weitz identifies as lacking in this period becomes a central motif in the fate of this protagonist. The film's opening appeal to identification ("Do you know what you'll be tomorrow?!") immediately pulls the viewer into a precarious situation, demanding an active engagement with his representative fate. Yet our capacity for empathy is hereby tested. For if the porter represents the old—his appearance clearly evoking Prussian militarism—then by seeing his humiliation as deserved we align ourselves with those who are coldhearted and cruel. However, if we take pity on him as a representative of the old order, are we thereby rejecting progress and modernity along with the new freedoms and possibilities that come with them? The film's complexities and contradictions may be too easily smoothed over by such allegorization, but the transitional moment with which it grapples cannot be understood in isolation from the historical realities that indelibly mark the year of its production and release. We will thus need to return to the alignment of the porter with this transition and how it affects our interpretation of his character and fate—and the film as a whole.

But it is equally important that we consider Murnau's film in terms of its form and style, which are bound up with the transformations in the German film industry at this time. 1924 was as much a transitional year for the young Weimar Republic culturally and aesthetically, particularly in cinema, as it was politically and economically. Of course, these realms cannot be fully isolated from one another, as we will see. Yet it is critical to our analysis of *The Last Laugh* that the film was made just as the tides were turning away from the Expressionism that had dominated the art cinema of the immediate postwar years to the more sober style of the latter half of the 1920s, which would be called *Neue Sachlichkeit*, "New Objectivity" or "New Sobriety." A witness to this shift, Murnau's film embodies the transition thematically and stylistically, mobilizing features that show its indebtedness to the trends of the previous half decade as well as anticipating new modes of perception that would be explored in its second half.[31]

It is difficult to speak of any clearly defined aesthetic programs in the cinema of this period. Expressionism, as it was developed in the non-cinematic visual arts and then in literature in the first decades of the twentieth century, had by the end of the war already nearly run its course. What has come to be known as Expressionism in film did not share the programmatic impulses or philosophical underpinnings of the pre-war movement, though it drew on many of that movement's key stylistic and thematic tropes: from the distortion and deformation of the natural world to angular compositions and stark contrasts, from the pronounced play of light and shadow to the use of characters who function as types, their anguish and struggles articulating universal conditions. Many of the films made from 1919 to 1924 that aimed to exploit this aesthetic are populated by eerie doubles, ghosts, or monsters, revealing a world haunted, if not by the supernatural, then by fears and anxieties that blur the boundaries between reality and dream, between this world and a fantastical one.

On the one hand, Murnau's early works clearly belong to this trend. The dominant themes of his films from this period, as Anton Kaes writes, are "fear, haunting, dream, horror, plague and death."[32] On the other hand, these story elements aside, his formal and visual vocabularies are less easy to classify. Murnau made relatively little use of the highly stylized, artificial, and abstract set designs that characterized films by Robert Wiene, for instance, whose *Das Cabinet des Dr. Caligari* (The Cabinet of Dr. Caligari, 1920) was one of the first—and unquestionably the most influential—works of Expressionist cinema. This lack of the signature off-kilter facades and painted shadows—referred to at the time as "Caligarism"—leads Thomas Elsaesser to caution against identifying Murnau the *stylist* with the other practitioners of cinematic Expressionism: "In so far as Murnau's films are 'Expressionist' at all, . . . they qualify less by their visual style than by their stories."[33]

How, then, to describe Murnau's distinctive style, so central to his achievement? His early films are suffused with an atmosphere of the uncanny and the otherworldly; even his simple shots of nature, as Kaes notes, can feel threatening.[34] Murnau achieves this atmosphere with a distinctive lighting and framing of claustrophobic interiors that reflect and heighten the anxiety and affliction of its trapped characters. A number of these features have been linked to the *Kammerspiel* tradition. In the *Kammerspielfilm* or chamber-play film, both the fantastical story elements and the contorted sets that distinguish the more overtly Expressionist films of the period largely fade away in favor of a more naturalistic portrayal of psychological conflict. Inspired by the softly lit, intimate productions of theater director Max Reinhardt (with whom Murnau worked in the 1910s), in which ambiance and subtle gesture convey characters' complexities, the *Kammerspielfilm* transfers the suffering and oppressiveness others had located in the nightmarish landscapes of the psyche into the everyday realm of the domestic sphere. It trades the distorted décor characteristic of the tales of horror and psychosis for comparatively plain, sparse interiors, typically populated by downtrodden and marginal figures from the lower class or petit bourgeoisie. It also minimizes title cards (when not dispensing with them entirely), profiting from the unity of time and space, along with enclosed spaces and a small cast, to tell a story through body language and atmosphere.

A number of Murnau's early films—especially *Der Gang in die Nacht* (Journey into the Night, 1921), *Schloss Vogelöd* (The Haunted Castle, 1921), *Der brennende Acker* (The Burning Soil, 1922), and *Phantom* (1922)—share more affinities with this trend in the art film of the period than with the full-blown Expressionist works of Karl Heinz Martin, Paul Wegener, or Artur Robison.[35] The comparatively realistic turn that characterized the *Kammerspielfilm* was nonetheless a limited one, shaped as it was by stylistic devices (e.g., chiaroscuro lighting) taken from the Expressionist toolbox. These films' set designs may be less distorted and unreal, their represented spaces more recognizable, even naturalistic, but these are still oppressive spaces that evoke much the same anxiety and anguish. This similarity is largely because these films are the products of the same studios and often the same group of artists. In fact, as Elsaesser has shown, the idea of "Expressionism" in the Weimar film world ultimately functioned mainly as a "brand-name" for the art cinema being produced at the time. It is thus more accurate to associate it not with any fixed aesthetic program or generic markers but with an arsenal of effects and themes whose common denominator is the people who used them, "a remarkably tight knit community of professionals—no more than two dozen names—operating as teams and skills networks."[36] These professionals included, among others, producer Erich Pommer, set designers Robert Herlth and Walter Röhrig, cameraman Karl Freund, and screenwriter Carl Mayer, all of whom worked on *The Last Laugh.*

But *The Last Laugh* does more than simply implement this arsenal of effects and themes in another variation of the *Kammerspielfilm*, however much it may have been conceived according to this model.[37] For although it was, following *Scherben* and *Sylvester*, the third film in a thematic trilogy that Carl Mayer had planned, Murnau and his team were seeking to craft a new look and new tone for the picture.[38] As Lotte Eisner notes, "visually and dramatically Murnau goes much further [in *The Last Laugh*], breaking out of the strict framework of the bourgeois *Kammerspiel*."[39] These ambitions for novelty aside, the new look of *The Last Laugh* would in part be determined by forces beyond Murnau's control: by 1924, the art film that had defined the German style since the war was fading, as a new, realistic vision began to assert itself. Eisner quotes film critics Raymond Borde and Freddy Buache, who plainly state that, "from 1924 on, there was a current of realism in Germany which took social observation as its object. *Kammerspiel* and metaphysics were soon swept away."[40] Thus, although *The Last Laugh* shares features with this subset of domestic dramas, Murnau transforms Mayer's *Kammerspiel* scenario into a work that explores and expands on the changes already underway in the film industry.[41] Erich Pommer, who had his finger on the pulse of the changing times, sensed that this was his chance to swing the doors in another direction. During the shooting of *The Last Laugh*, Pommer told Murnau and his team: "Please invent something new, even if it's crazy!"[42]

A financial reason also factored into the shift in the young republic's aesthetic temperament, especially in cinema: the German film industry wanted to expand its appeal beyond working-class audiences to a broader public. As Marc Silberman explains, while the "art cinema produced in Germany provided the industry with a distinct image of cultural legitimacy which became a competitive factor both for domestic and international audiences," it was not really commercially successful, because it did "not appeal to a mass audience."[43] In fact, it was the unstable economy and increasing inflation of 1919 to 1923 that made possible these otherwise commercially questionable productions: "Inflation favored … the export of German films because they were relatively cheap on the international market and … protected the domestic market from imports because foreign production companies could not earn enough from distribution in Germany." As Silberman notes, *The Last Laugh* was the final prestige production by Ufa that was able to take advantage of this volatile market and profit from international distribution. By the end of 1924, the German film industry was beginning to accommodate the "shift in audience demands for more realism" as it also dealt with competition on two fronts: the increased prevalence of American productions and the novel media of radio.[11]

This change in economic circumstances and audience demands coincided with a trend away from the metaphysical excesses of Expressionism, which sought truths hidden beneath the surface of things, to a more sober and exacting look at that surface. *The Last Laugh* was born at the crossroads of these stylistic tendencies, which are also mapped onto the divide constitutive of the story itself, the divide between the old and the new. The old is situated in the dark and dusty tenement building, the space of the working class, whose stifling interiors become the actual and metaphorical locus of struggle. The new, starting around 1924, was the reaction against Expressionism that came to be known as New Objectivity. This was a movement fascinated by much that the Expressionists feared, in particular the machinery of modern urban life, the proliferation of novel objects and gadgets, and the brilliant displays of light that drew attention to facades and the exteriors of persons and things. New Objectivity called for a return to a cool and critical attitude to modernity in all its forms. Artists attempted to reveal the matter at hand (*die Sache*) without embellishment and with precision. If the Expressionist aesthetic shapes the oppressive shadows and drudgery of the tenement courtyard in *The Last Laugh*, the impetus to be dazzled by surface displays of reflecting light can be seen in the film's shots of the hotel, with its huge glass windows and bright open spaces, and in the big city where it is situated, with its unending flow of cars and people amid flashing lights.[45]

Ultimately, however, the strict division of old (Expressionist-derived *Kammerspielfilm*, constricted interiors) and new (realistic explorations of urban expanse and mass culture) is not so easily upheld in *The Last Laugh*, which makes it a fascinating case study as a transitional film that draws on various modes of representation.

Complicating matters more, New Objectivity was also drawn to the flipside of modern consumerist culture. Poverty, prostitution, and other realities of life in the big city were sought out and depicted *as such*, not, as in Expressionist works, fetishized into ciphers of some hidden truth. Thus in the second half of the 1920s, the *Straßenfilm* or "street film" of the Weimar period, inaugurated with Karl Grune's *Die Straße* (The Street, 1923) and developed most famously by G. W. Pabst in *Die freudlose Gasse* (Joyless Street, 1925), sought to turn a more sober eye at these aspects of urban living. In many ways, Murnau's portrayal of the lower-class tenements more closely resembles these films' subdued, realistic representations of the working class. It is the hotel, in contrast, that becomes the site of haunted hallways and constricted spaces; and it is in the hotel's washroom, layered with oblique shadows, where the porter eventually succumbs. Indeed, as we will see, the most direct allusion to the Expressionist aesthetic in the film arrives in the dream sequence, which plays out in a version of the hotel.

In the street films of the period, the bustling thoroughfares represent the open space of seduction and danger that characters confront once they have broken out of their confined interiors (*Kammerspielfilm*) or psyches (Expressionist film). In *The Last Laugh*, the street simultaneously separates and connects these worlds. It is both threshold and juncture, the unpredictable space of movement and change. The porter at first oversees this realm of urban transition. And although his decline forces him into the static space of the subterranean washroom, Murnau eventually reinstalls him, not to his post, but as a traveler on the very street whose comings and goings he had previously regulated. Thus we see him in the film's final shot as he sets off down the street in a carriage, heading away from both tenement and hotel.

Jannings's doorman stands at the threshold of worlds just as this film assumes a place on the threshold of new cinematic possibilities, neither firmly rooted in one or the other, but making possible the transfer and cross-pollination of ideas and images emerging from one and disappearing into the other. Where he "belongs," in the end, is unclear. Ostensibly at home in the tenement, he is rejected by its denizens. At first seemingly master of the metropolitan space that the upscale hotel represents, he ends up being subjugated by it. Only in the epilogue does he find freedom from both spaces—though that freedom seems ultimately to be an illusion. Caught between these realms, precariously at home in neither, the porter embodies the tensions and unresolved contradictions of the young Weimar Republic at its moment of transition. In order to convey this moment as one of uncertain change, Murnau oscillates between and blends visual modes, at times situating old motifs in new spaces, at others trying out novel ideas within the conventions he inherited. The result is a spectacular fusion of styles at the crossroads of aesthetic regimes that also demanded innovative techniques to achieve. Pushing the capabilities of Ufa studios to their limits, Murnau and his team sought not just to tell a simple story with big implications but also to expand the scope of cinema itself, to introduce a new mode of seeing (lead cinematographer Karl Freund called it "ein neues optisches Sehen") that would alter the viewer's experience of filmic space.[46]

Activating Cinematic Space

Indeed, it is space rather than time—the latter usually considered cinema's privileged purview—that becomes key to both story and theme in *The Last Laugh*. The ways in which Murnau and Freund open up and explore cinematic space transform the film's interiors, backdrops, and architecture, the realms in or against which its events unfold, into important actors. Space itself is essentially the second main character in the film, so that, as one scholar writes, it becomes the "productive site of the drama," the characters serving only as "attributes."[47]

This special emphasis on space becomes apparent in the first few shots of the film. After the title card and epigraph comes a cut to black that lasts over three full seconds. Rather than providing a brief caesura before the film proper, this longer-than-usual blank screen actually has a mimetic referent, as we learn once the first light appears on the screen. For indeed, this light enters the frame from below moving upward to fill the screen and reveal a view from an elevator descending to the lobby of a hotel (figs. 2 and 3). The extended black at the beginning of the shot, therefore, conveys the darkness of the elevator shaft before the elevator emerges into the main lobby. The first thing the viewer sees in the film's diegesis is in fact an obscured view; the first few seconds of black are therefore not a blank screen but a shot of the dark metal shaft blocking the lobby's light. Before seeing anything, then, we experience the inability to see at all. This blindness, it turns out, is one of the film's central concerns.

As the camera continues downward with the elevator, we see the front of the caged shaft as it moves past, creating a pattern of vertical and horizonal bars that crisscross the lobby floor in the distance. These patterns include another stretch of opaque metal that entirely obstructs the view of the lobby, effectively blacking out the frame in a way that echoes the opening seconds. The rhythms created by the alternation of light and dark moving from the bottom of the frame to the top not only mimic the (actual) descent of the elevator. They also recall the mechanism of the cinematic projector, which displays images by way of the vertical movement of the film strip, frame by frame, each image interrupted by shutter blackout. This opening shot announces that *The Last Laugh* is as much a film about the cinematic apparatus and its affordances as it is about a "last man" who was once "the first," though of course the descent of the camera also anticipates the downward trajectory of the porter from "first" to "last."[48]

Figure 2. Opening shot: descent in the elevator resembling film strip with shutter blackout.

Figure 3. Opening shot: view of the hotel lobby from the elevator, with revolving door at the far end.

As the elevator reaches the ground floor, the vertical path of the descent becomes a horizontal movement into the open space of the lobby, first by way of the opening of the elevator doors, and then by means of the camera's advance into this space, mimicking the steps of the hotel guests by crossing from the confined enclosure of the lift into the hotel's capacious entry and waiting area, across which it proceeds gracefully to glide, approaching and then halting at the wide and tall glass doors at the other end of the lobby. In the surviving versions of the film, a cut interrupts what was originally a single, seamless take,[49] a cinematographic overture of sorts, an uninterrupted mobile sweep from on high, through crowded space, and up to a threshold. Even with the cut, the effect is exhilarating. As the camera moves in and comes to rest, we find ourselves in a position similar to the one in which the take—and the film—started, facing a glass barrier, one through which we are afforded a vista on yet another bustling space, the street outside, which is marked by both horizontal and vertical movement, the former created by the cars and people passing, the latter by the pouring rain. But it is not just the space beyond the doors that is in motion. The main entrance itself, a revolving door, is turning in circles, so that although the camera has now come to rest, the frame through which we see the world continues perpetually to move (fig. 4). Much like what the cinematic apparatus both reveals and instantiates—the circular spinning door being a stand-in for the ever-revolving film reel—both the world and our window on it remain in flux.[50]

This frame-within-a-frame of the revolving door demarcates and at the same time opens up space. In the first place it allows a view onto the street and into the city beyond, which extends far back, the depth of field revealing multiple densely packed and crisscrossing layers of urban commotion. Murnau created this effect by using increasingly larger cars in the stratified foreground and moving cutouts of smaller people and automobiles in the receding background. As set designer Robert Herlth recalls,

Figure 4. End of opening shot: camera lingers on the revolving door, here both frame and reflecting surface.

the view . . . seen from the revolving door was managed by means of a perspective shot of a sloping street 15 metres high in the foreground diminishing to 5 in the "distance." The street ran between model skyscrapers as much as 17 metres high. . . . To make the "perspective" work we had big buses and Mercedes cars in the foreground; in the middle-ground middle-sized cars; and in the background small ones, with behind them again children's toy cars. Farthest away of all, in front of the shops, we had crowds of "people" cut out and painted and moved across the screen on a conveyor belt.[51]

Herlth's description of the depth perspective afforded by the four layers with correspondingly sized vehicles and people (foreground, middle-ground, background, and behind the background) does not fully capture the extent to which these strata are multiplied by the crossing in both directions of numerous vehicles, creating the impression that there are up to nine layers in the receding cityscape. In fact, a sketch of the plan for this perspectival feat drawn by Herlth and Walter Röhrig reveals exactly this number of distinct paths for cars and people between the doorman and the facade of buildings at the far end of the visual field (fig. 6).

This shot through the revolving door—we are still dealing here with the first shot of the film!—also points back to the space inside the hotel, which the camera has just surveyed as it made its way down to and across the lobby to the entrance, and which is equally characterized by constant movement.[52] For reflected in the continually gyring glass panes are the electric lights of the hotel interior, which flicker and fade, flashing and flitting by as the glass moves (visible in the middle of the frame, fig. 4). Against the deep focus of the light-spottled cityscape with its mesh of zig-zagging pedestrians and vehicles, the resulting patterns of light and dark have an almost kaleidoscopic effect. After the rain stops, Murnau places the camera on the other side of the revolving door, using the wet pavement as a further reflective surface for the play of lights. Elsaesser describes the multiplied reflections afforded by the rain and its aftermath as allowing "for the light to catch itself once more in the wet, glistening folds of the doorman's capacious oilskin, before Jannings takes it off to reveal the shimmering gold braid and buttons of his livery."[53]

Nested framings similar to the one used in this opening shot— which is itself frequently reprised—can be found throughout the film, though they just as often restrict space as open it up. Murnau repeatedly situates the viewer behind a window or door, often keeping the action at a distance, drawing attention to the framing of the shot, which is doubled in the diegesis by way of the rectangular outline of the respective opening. The second shot of the film, for example, maintains the frame-within-a-frame composition of the preceding one, placing the spectator on the street outside the hotel with a view

Figure 5. On-set photograph showing the cityscape illusion. Source: Stiftung Deutsche Kinemathek.

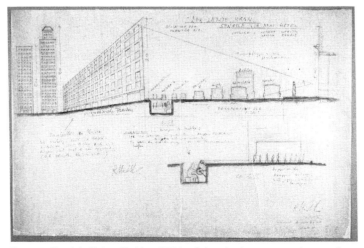

Figure 6. Sketch by Robert Herlth and Walter Röhrig for the view across the street from the hotel entrance, with receding skyline in the background. Mechanism for moving silhouettes at bottom center-right. Source: La Cinémathèque française.

of the entrance from an angle opposite that of the previous shot. But here it is not the same revolving door seen from the other side that at first fills the screen. Rather, the shot begins with a perspective through the partially lowered window of a cab that has just arrived. Right above the glass we see the face of Jannings as the porter, visible in its entirety for the first time (fig. 7). As the cab pulls away, the hotel entrance is fully revealed with a wide view of its glass windows and doors, and beyond these the lobby we had just left, including the elevator beginning its ascent.

Such transparent or semi-transparent barriers, particularly glass doors and windows inside the hotel, serve both dramatic and thematic purposes. Murnau makes so much use of transparent divisions in the mise-en-scène that one critic calls him "a Mies van der Rohe of film."[54] These are structures that cut up space in peculiar ways,

Figure 7. Second shot: Jannings framed through a cab window.

allowing for the spectator's gaze to cross over while still prohibiting easy physical movement. This traversal across the glass boundary is the purview of our protagonist. When we first meet him, he is fully in control of the transparent threshold, master of the liminal space between worlds, facilitating the transfer of people and objects in and out of the luxury hotel. In losing his post at this demarcating space, the porter also loses the natural ease with which he is able to co-exist in the worlds on either side of the line. After his demotion he will have to cross this boundary with illicit goods (his stolen uniform). Among the unsuitable hotel guests who will then have to be turned away is the porter himself. Ironically, after being banished from the liminal zone he is also banished by his family, so that the only place he has to go is the hotel, the world to which he does not belong. That he ends up wasting away in the bowels of the hotel is ultimately so shameful, because it exposes the divide that, in his former role, he had so assiduously helped both to maintain and to obscure.

The hotel itself is marked as a liminal space by way of its name, Atlantic, which refers to the ocean that divides the old world from the new. That separation of old and new, a central theme of the film, expresses a division that is generational as well as socioeconomic.[55] Murnau elevates this division to a near-mythic status. If the Atlantic Ocean is the "sea of Atlas," then the porter carries the heavens on his shoulders like the mythic Greek god. When we first meet him, he is literally protecting people from the heavens, holding an umbrella (prominently featuring the name "Atlantic") to keep the guests from getting drenched in the downpour. Yet he also carries the bags of the bourgeoisie on his shoulders, an ironic commentary on his subservient role in relation to his self-image. As this image of himself collapses, the world around him becomes more threatening. Once the porter loses his position, he is unable to protect even himself from the heavens falling in on him: leaving the Atlantic with his stolen uniform, he cowers as the hotel appears to topple over onto him (fig. 8). What holds a building up are its structures of support, sometimes shaped as men in an architectural design known as "atlantes" (plural of Atlas). Although these load-bearing gods flank the Atlantic hotel's entrance (fig. 9), they are clearly not structural at all, but only ornamental. Is Jannings's doorman, ultimately, any different?

This question is raised by the demotion of the porter, which sets the film's action in motion, fundamentally altering his and our perception of the liminal spaces the numerous glass barriers represent. This scene unfolds behind the mullioned double doors of the manager's office. But Murnau starts at a distance, only gradually taking the viewer increasingly closer, crossing key borders along the way, until we read, with the doorman's eyes, the critical line from his letter of demotion: "The reason for this measure is your decrepitude [*Altersschwäche*]." The scene begins with a wide shot of the lobby. The porter is in the center of the frame, though he appears as a mere speck in the background, the smallest human figure in the shot, mostly obscured behind the doors on the far side of the lobby and then eclipsed by the guests walking past in the foreground (fig. 10). The shot shows him as he feels at that moment: barely significant to the goings-on in the hotel and nearly invisible. Cut to a full shot of those doors, behind which we see the porter, standing in the right half, and in the left half the manager, seated (fig. 11). Murnau holds this shot for a long time before passing over the barrier. First the camera rolls up to and then (with a dissolve) through the glass to a medium close-up of our protagonist reading the letter. Then, as if breaking through this solid architectural boundary were not enough, the camera crosses the divide between object and subject, "practically leaping into the porter," as one critic puts it, to show us, from his perspective and with his affective response, the minute details of the letter.[56] Over this close-up of the typed letter, a masked oval opens up to show—in what I take to be a scene playing out in the porter's imagination— the old washroom attendant, whose place Jannings's character will now take, being relieved of his services. Finally, after a brief cut back

Figure 8. Falling hotel: the building itself threatens to collapse.

Figure 9. Atlantes (statues of men holding up the lights) outside the "Atlantic"—will they keep the hotel from falling?

Figure 10. Wide shot of lobby with the porter behind closed doors at the far end of the visual field, center.

Figure 11. Full shot of mullioned doors: scene of demotion.

to an external view of the disbelieving porter adjusting his glasses, we get an extreme close-up of each word in the key sentence of the letter and then, slowly, of the letters in the word "*A l t e r s s c h w ä c h e*," which become blurry as the old man struggles to comprehend what is happening to him, tears presumably welling in his eyes.[57]

Perhaps Murnau lingers for over a minute of screen time on the full shot of the porter from behind the glass in order to prepare his viewers—to sharpen their visual and spatial sensitivity—for the crossings of boundaries that follow. And yet, in heightening the effect of those tricks of the mobile camera, he also draws attention to the porter's immobility. For although the mullions and bars of the doors and windows at first resemble a painter's grid, as if the event unfolding on the other side were being marked as worthy of artistic rendering, of being fixed on the canvas, they soon become markers of imprisonment and enclosure.[58] As the camera smoothly and effortlessly crosses the threshold, we realize that it has more freedom than Jannings's character will now ever have. Indeed, in subsequent shots the former porter will appear behind these and other doors as if trapped, caught in the crosshairs, and desperate to find a way out (figs. 12 and 13). In these moments, the modern urban hotel's putative efficiency and transparency reveal their inherent cruelties, its interiors reminiscent of the confined spaces found in the *Kammerspielfilm*.

The difference is that these are not opaque and squalid spaces, but rather vitreous and spectral ones that participate in the hotel's intricate play of light. Here is the sinister flipside of its numerous lustrous and transparent partitions. Pier Giorgio Tone reads the film's reflective surfaces, especially its mirrors (the one at home, the pocket mirror, and the washroom mirror), as constantly reaffirming the doorman's alienation, at once providing "images of who the protagonist wants to be and must be," while also standing in for "his profound loneliness and his enclosure in oppressive spaces."[59] Unlike the two mirrors in which he coiffes himself, however, the prominent

Figures 12 and 13. Behind the barrier of the hotel's interior glass doors (*left*); in the crosshairs (*right*).

wall of mirrors in the washroom does not offer an idealized image of the ex-porter, who instead appears in it as a displaced double, his alienated self as "other" (fig. 14). The doorman's demotion to the washroom may be, as Lotte Eisner writes, akin to a "descent into Hell,"[60] but the washroom itself is not your typical infernal pit. Murnau presents it in an unholy blend of anguished *Kammerspiel* confinement and New Objectivist surface reflection, juxtaposing the prison-like shadows of this narrow, underground space with the spotlessness of its gleaming marble and lights, which, in contrast, appear grotesque.[61]

The mirror-doubled ex-porter in the washroom echoes an earlier scene, right before his demotion, in which he first spies his uniformed replacement assuming his post. Just as Jannings's character moves through the revolving door from the outside in, a new porter moves through it from the inside out. The old man gapes at this figure as if the glass panes were playing a trick on him. Inside the reflective rotating door the new porter appears as if he were a double, an idealized version of the old man, stronger and younger, like what he sees in his mirrors.[62] Stephen Brockmann writes that it is "as if part of the doorman's personality, the one he is most proud of, had been cut away from him."[63] This "cut away" doppelgänger has been so flawlessly integrated into the machinery of the hotel that

Figure 14. Alienated ex-porter reflected in the mirror.

Figure 15. The porter's doppelgänger in the revolving door.

he assumes its lustrous characteristics, casting his own reflection in the glass in an image not of alienation or idealization, but of perfect symmetry (fig. 15).

The revolving door is the site where many of the ambiguities and tensions we found in the hotel's glass partitioning and mirrors come together. It is both solid and transparent, simultaneously barrier and opening. But unlike the other doors in the hotel, its movement in one direction always also includes an equivalent movement in the other. As one person enters, another is forced out. As such it becomes a trope for the wheel of fortune in which the porter is caught, as is made explicit in the shot that shows him entering as the new porter exits, their positions effectively swapped out. Siegfried Kracauer describes the revolving door in *The Last Laugh* as "something between a merry-go-round and a roulette wheel."[64] Both devices belong to the realm of play, though in the latter case chance determines whether you win or lose. The ease and inevitability with which fate "turns" on the porter, however, do not seem attributable to the workings of chance so much as to an inescapable shift brought about by the cycle of life. That life keeps going, that the wheel keeps turning, is expressed in the door's mechanical regularity and predictability (so unlike the roulette wheel). It is the steady and unstoppable comings and goings of modern urban living more than its randomness that Murnau conveys with this central architectural image—though he will allow chance to intervene in the tacked-on ending. The continually rotating door moreover suggests finality in its efficient replacement of the porter, the way it takes him in and spits him out, ejecting him from the privileged sphere above into that of the washroom below where, in the end, he will meet the fate of his predecessor and be expunged from the sphere of labor altogether (the old washroom attendant is transferred to a nursing home).[65]

To be swallowed up in this way by the perpetually rotating door evokes a more turbulent image of centripetal motion. Elsewhere in his study of Weimar cinema, Kracauer locates such a force in the whirlpool, an image he uses to describe the chaos that, he argues, is symbolized in the circular motifs found throughout the films of the era.[66] This image of the vortex combines the fateful inevitability expressed by Murnau's revolving door with the notions of instability and confusion. Now the ineluctable force and "permanent motion" of this door can also be seen as a form of whirling chaos that will only end in the deadly vacuum at its center.[67] The regularity and finality suggested by *The Last Laugh*'s revolving door thus overlap in Kracauer's whirlpool motif with the disorienting and destabilizing experience of modernity characteristic of the early Weimar Republic. Kracauer of course had the hindsight to see where this particular transitional moment would end, that its maelstrom would indeed turn out to be utterly ineluctable.

The Unchained Camera

The movement within the cinematic frame afforded by the staged bustle of urban life, the ascent and descent of the elevator, and the revolving door is complemented by the innovative mobile camera of Karl Freund, a critical ingredient in this new, dynamic space. The importance of Freund's camerawork both for this film and for film history is hard to exaggerate. As mentioned at the book's start, prior to *The Last Laugh* the cinematographic apparatus never left the tripod. Camera movement, when used at all, was made possible by occasional tilts and pans as well as, in certain contexts, by mounting the apparatus onto an already mobile vehicle. These latter experiments gave rise to the popular "phantom ride" films of the turn of the century, in which cameras were fixed to a moving train, trolly, carriage, automobile, or boat to create a point-of-view experience. This technique can be found in some features as well. Lupu Pick's *Scherben* (1921), for instance, includes shots slowly tracking a character from behind as he walks on a train track, the camera presumably atop a handcar. Murnau used similar short tracking shots in *The Burning Soil* (from a horse-drawn carriage and a sleigh) and *Nosferatu* (from a ship), both from the year after *Scherben*. In the dance scene in *Phantom*, also from 1922, the camera assumes a character's perspective briefly for a spinning shot of a room, though this was likely achieved by means of pans and tilts.[68]

Since these shots made use of existing modes of transportation, they were limited to the streets, rails, and waterways where these vehicles were in use. Creating similar tracking shots on a studio set was not so easy. The 1910s and 1920s, however, also saw some limited and isolated experiments in which a wheeled platform was constructed for the express purpose of making travelling shots, though most of these were relatively brief and consisted of slow track-ins. Giovanni Pastrone's *Cabiria* (1914) was the first feature film more prominently to use a primitive dolly for tracking shots. The travelling shots in this epic are quite unlike the phantom ride shorts, however, since they are gradual and unobtrusive. Carl Mayer, screenwriter of both *The Last Laugh* and *Sylvester*, claimed that the first use of a dolly in Germany was in the latter, 1923 Pick feature, where a few of the street scenes (including one of the opening shots) include a travelling camera moving slowly on the main drag. Yet, as Katharina Loew points out, brief tracking shots can be found in Germany even earlier, such as in Lubitsch's *Die Augen der Mumie Ma* (The Eyes of the Mummy Ma) from 1918.[69] Nonetheless, Mayer appears to be the main source of the mobile shots in *Sylvester* and *The Last Laugh*. Indeed, they clearly emerge from the same desire to create a purely visual feature, perhaps as compensation for the paucity of text.[70]

In *The Last Laugh*, however, Freund goes well beyond what Mayer had asked for in *Sylvester* the year before, when, rolling platform aside, the camera remained firmly fixed to the tripod.[71] Compared to the barely perceptible drift of the frame in Pick's film and in earlier experiments with travelling shots in films like *Cabiria*, the movements in *The Last Laugh* are bold and provocative. Inspired by Mayer and

Murnau's vision, Freund expands the potential for camera movement much further than it had ever been taken before, not only employing more (and swifter) travelling shots but also by fully "unchaining" the camera from the tripod. Thus freed, the camera could be strapped to the cameraman's chest (fig. 16), placed in a basket with a hoist, put on rails, or otherwise made to swoop through space, made newly accessible in all its depth and complexity through these and related techniques. The camera floats through the halls and corridors of the hotel, stumbles when the porter loses his grip, begins to spin in a dizzying circle when he becomes intoxicated, and flies from mouth to ear as gossip spreads among the tenement women.

Freund tended to embellish when discussing the actual means used for some of these shots in order to stress the innovation of the "unchained camera" (*entfesselte Kamera*), which became a catch phrase at the time. In one of the most commonly repeated anecdotes, Freund claims to have attached the camera to a bicycle for the travelling opening shot of the film.[72] Yet, as Luciano Berriatúa has shown, we can see Freund in a chair in the reflection of the revolving glass door, suggesting that instead of a cumbersome bicycle setup, he simply put his camera on a platform with wheels.[73] Katharina Loew rightly notes that critics often conflate tracking shots, tilts, pans, and other movements that are possible with the camera still fixed to the tripod with the "unchained camera."[74] Although the distinction is important, what makes *The Last Laugh* so innovative is not only that it was the first to experiment with a truly unchained camera but that it also made ample use of existing techniques for camera movement. Thus, even when it remained fixed to the tripod, as in the opening shot of the film, the range, variation, and artfulness Freund brought to the possible movements of the camera exceeded anything that had been done before, seemingly removing all limitations on its formal creativity.

Beyond demonstrating—however dazzlingly—an impressive new dimension of cinematic form, the mobile camera serves a number of

Figure 16. On set: Karl Freund with camera strapped to his chest. Murnau is standing to his left. Source: Stiftung Deutsche Kinemathek.

novel narrative purposes in *The Last Laugh*. For one, it visually conveys sound, a feature of the world otherwise absent from the silent pictures of the period. When the bugle player performs in the tenement courtyard after the wedding, for example, Freund shows us how his music reaches the porter, still up in the apartment, by means of a shot that swiftly swoops out and up from an extreme close-up of the horn's bell to a high-angle long shot of the player and his companion below.[75] The angle and distance correspond to the relative position of the porter, whom we see standing at the open window listening in the next shot. Production designer Robert Herlth describes the mechanism by which they were able "to represent a sound travelling through space": "We ... fitted Jannings's house with a sort of hoist, with the camera in a basket on rails, so that it could slide downward for about 20 metres, i.e., from Jannings's ear to the bell of the horn."[76]

Figure 17. On-set photograph showing how the "flying horn sound" shot was achieved. Source: Stiftung Deutsche Kinemathek.

Because this shot does not travel "downward" but rather upward, and such a movement would have been difficult, the film must have been reversed.[77] An on-set picture shows the contraption that was used (fig. 17). Other photographs from the set (figs. 18 and 19) give clues to how a similar shot was achieved for the gossip scene, likely also using reversed footage. Here the camera mimics the women's voices travelling from one balcony to the next, first with a fast pan and tilt, and then with a shot that moves in from a medium framing of a woman located on the top floor of the building to a close-up of her hand at her ear, listening.

Although the unchained camera does a lot of narrative and descriptive work, not to mention expanding cinema's formal palette, it also alters the viewing experience in a more subtle yet fundamental way that results in a transformed perception of the filmic world. Its invention is a turning point in the history of cinema that dramatically shifts the emphasis of the medium from conveying time and the

Figure 18. Production photograph showing a rig constructed for the travelling camera shots on the tenement courtyard set. Source: Stiftung Deutsche Kinemathek.

experience of temporality to conveying space and spatiality.[78] Although these realms cannot be entirely separated in cinema, filmic movement prior to the mobile camera principally indexed the passing of time. Limited as it was to the static frame, movement was strictly pro-filmic, consisting of the actions unfolding in front of the fixed camera. The innovation of the *moving* picture (we still call them "movies") correlated precisely to this temporal dimension, which, unlike the still photograph, captured the world in flux, displaying it with the illusion of actual motion (film still consists of a sequence of unmoving frames). The experience of the early cinema was a novel experience of this life-like movement in time. Film was seen as "the imprint of time itself."[79]

The mobile camera removes the barrier of the otherwise static frame that keeps all movement corralled within it by extending the scope of cinematic motion to the frame itself. This movement of

Figure 19. Production photograph showing the rig for floating camera shots. Source: Stiftung Deutsche Kinemathek.

the frame, which corresponds to the newly "unchained" apparatus, is fundamentally different from the illusion of motion made possible by the film projector's continual flicker of still images. Granting mobility to the image *as framed space* profoundly opens up a film's field of vision not simply by disclosing what is offscreen or out of the camera's focal range (which a cut to a new shot could easily afford) but by advancing *into* the spaces outside its immediate purview, thereby also extending the four boundaries of the usually fixed frame. For this reason, Freund's innovation in freeing the camera from the tripod is more than just a technical feat with stylistic consequences. The mobile camera in *The Last Laugh* alters the cinematic experience on a more elemental level. Besides being able to represent time in an unprecedented way, film is now also free to explore space, placing the viewer in a dynamic relation to the pro-filmic world. The camera becomes both a new eye and a new body, capable of traversing the three-dimensional realms depicted on the screen.

In this way, Freund's mobile camera inaugurates cinema's most radical break from the other visual arts (including drama), making *The Last Laugh* the first full realization of the medium's true potential— one might even say the beginning of modern cinema as such. Indeed, its impact was immediate and has proved to be enduring: today, films *without* camera movement are the aberration. During the filming of *The Last Laugh*, a young Alfred Hitchcock was on a set nearby in Babelsberg (for the joint British-Ufa production *The Blackguard*, which he had co-written). Hitchcock visited Murnau's set and was duly impressed, as his subsequent experimentation with tracking shots attests. Indeed, a tracking shot appears in the opening sequence of his first feature, *The Pleasure Garden*, filmed in Munich one year after *The Last Laugh*.[80] The latter half of the 1920s saw an explosion of moving-camera experiments, most inspired by Freund's work on this Murnau picture. Freund himself went on to use and develop these techniques in films by other directors, most notably Fritz Lang's *Metropolis* (1927) and even later, in Hollywood, Todd Browning's

Dracula (1931) as well as, in the director's chair, *The Mummy* (1932). In many ways, the notion of the camera being "unchained" points beyond its actual detachment from the tripod to the new formal possibilities—Promethean creativity—that were unleashed in its wake.

It is no accident that buildings are central to this film in which space itself is opened up anew.[81] In a reflection on camera movement written prior to the filming of *The Last Laugh*, Murnau describes what he aims to achieve with the mobile camera as "the 'architectural' film." It is his wish that Father Christmas would bring for him "a camera that can move freely in space" (the wish turns out to be doubly prophetic, since *The Last Laugh* premiered two days before Christmas):

> What I mean is one that at any moment can go anywhere, at any speed. A camera that outstrips present film technique and fulfils the cinema's ultimate artistic goal. Only with this essential instrument shall we be able to realize new possibilities, including one of the most promising, the "architectural" film.
>
> What I refer to is the fluid architecture of bodies with blood in their veins moving through mobile space; the interplay of lines rising, falling, disappearing; the encounter of surfaces, stimulation and its opposite, calm; construction and collapse; the formation and destruction of a hitherto almost unsuspecting life; all this adds up to a symphony made up of the harmony of bodies and the rhythm of space; the *play of pure movement*, vigorous and abundant. All this we shall be able to create when the camera has at last been de-materialized.
>
> To attain this end we don't ask for some complicated new technical apparatus; what we ask for, and this precisely from the artistic point of view, is just the opposite: we want to return to a technical process that will be almost artistically sober and self-sufficient, creating a completely neutral medium which will lend itself freely to every new creation.[82]

Here Murnau articulates an avant-garde aesthetic that would not be out of place coming from Walter Ruttmann, who was experimenting with animated abstract shorts during this period (his *Opus* films were made between 1921 and 1925) but had not yet transposed his vision of film as a pure art of motion, "midway between painting and music," into the realm of live action.[83] He would achieve this vision in 1927 with *Berlin: Die Sinfonie der Großstadt* (Berlin: Symphony of a Metropolis), a work whose title refers to the same musical form to which Murnau appeals in his reverie of cinema as "*pure movement*." This is a movement that precedes and supersedes story and character. It is the realm of cinema as the space of form in motion. For Murnau, these forms consist of "bodies," "lines," and "surfaces"—abstract shapes whose "interplay" manifests in conflicting forces of "rising" and "falling," "stimulation" and "calm," "construction" and "collapse," as well as "formation" and "destruction." Murnau's vision of a "rhythm of space" is "architectural" in the sense that it traces out structural possibilities inherent in forms of life in terms of a unity of purpose. That purpose, however, is not habitation, but movement. The space opened by film is not so much where human interactions take place as it is where such interactions participate in a larger interplay of animated bodies.

This description of "the fluid architecture of bodies" in "mobile space" corresponds to the opening sequence of *The Last Laugh*, with its multiple trajectories of movement. It also anticipates the ways in which Murnau literally makes architecture mobile, most prominently in the revolving door and elevator. Indeed, without Murnau and Freund's experiments with the unchained camera, the radical experiments in Ruttmann's 1927 film (not incidentally also based on a Carl Mayer scenario and with Freund at the camera) would not have been possible (though that film's aesthetic derives more from montage than from camera movement). Murnau's call for the "dematerialization" of the camera is curious, however. What he requires for the "pure movement" of cinematic space is that the camera be "neutral," as if being grounded by the tripod forced a specific perspective from which the world had to be captured. Freed from its unmoving, fixed position, able "to go anywhere" "at any moment" and "at any speed" means the camera can be "sober" (a key concept for the New Objectivity of the latter half of the 1920s) and "self-sufficient" with respect to the world and can, ultimately, disappear in it.[84]

Thus the disembodied, "dematerialized" camera can hover and float through space in a way that the camera never could when it was chained to the tripod.[85] Its newfound mobility makes possible not only the virtuoso descent and seamless swoop of the film's first take but also the swift ascent of the "flying horn sound" shot. In this way, Murnau's dream of "dematerialization" applies not so much to the camera as to the frame, now a completely arbitrary limit on the space which the viewer not only sees but also inhabits. In occupying that space, the audience establishes a new visual relationship with the world that corresponds to the shifting social and urban experiences of the period. The camera-eye's newfound freedom grants spectators an "unregulated, value-free mode of seeing" whose agile movements evoke "the social mobility experienced in the Weimar years, both positively and negatively," confronting the dynamic spaces of modernity as sites of both fascination and danger.[86]

Intimations of Abstraction: The Dream Sequence

To further explore the affordances offered by the mobile camera we should examine its more radical implementation in the dream sequence and the drunken subjective shots that precede it. The "flying horn sound" shot discussed earlier sets in motion a series of highly inventive camera movements that begin by mimicking the experience of inebriation. After hearing this sound, our protagonist stumbles into a chair, and Murnau cuts to a medium close shot of him in an intoxicated state of bliss. The frame then begins to move,

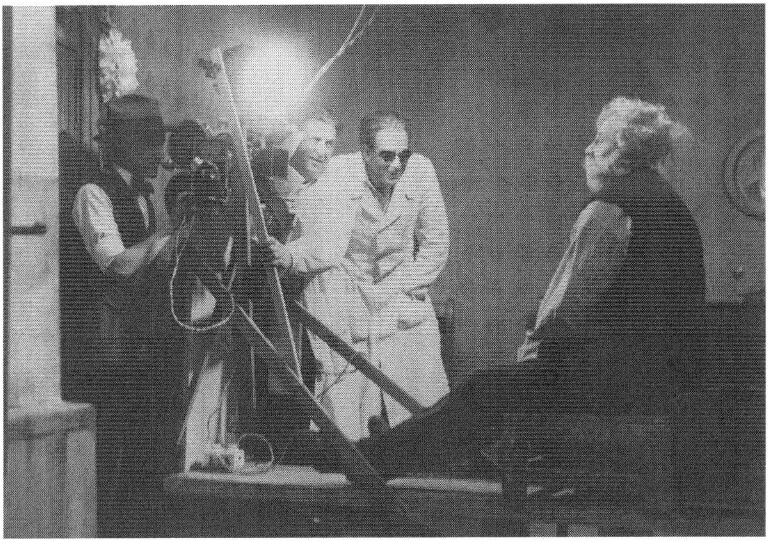

Figure 20. The spinning platform constructed for the drunken sequence. Karl Freund center; camera assistant Robert Baberske to his right; Murnau to his left. Source: Stiftung Deutsche Kinemathek.

sweeping first left and then right, the room behind the ex-porter appearing to spin around him as he remains fixed to the center of the frame. In fact, the effect was created by moving Jannings with the camera, as is revealed in a photograph from the set that shows the rotating platform Freund and Murnau constructed for this shot (fig. 20). The spinning lasts only a few dizzying seconds before a close-up of the ex-porter indicates that we will now assume his perspective. What follows is nearly unprecedented in the history of cinema. Freund has unmounted the camera, which now appears to be handheld. The ensuing twelve-second shot roams through the room, unsteadily and at times jerkily drifting about, now swerving left, now stumbling back, then lurching forward, before swiftly sweeping right.[87] The room becomes a blur. We can just make out the windows with curtains and the table laden with wine bottles, a credenza with a framed picture above it, and maybe an armchair.

By the end of this sequence, everything becomes a grey wash as the porter slips into sleep.

After we see the ex-porter begin to nod off, a final shot of the horn player shows the transition from inebriated wakefulness to soporific repose. With low lighting and soft focus, the camera shows the drunken player with horn to mouth, bell facing the camera. His companion is visible to his right. This image slowly becomes softer and softer, and as it loses focus the human figures disappear and the shiny horn bell starts to distort and double, casting patterns of light in a near-kaleidoscopic play of abstract shapes (fig. 21). The dissolution of clearly definable objects in the real world inventively captures the gradual loss of consciousness experienced by the doorman as he hears the postnuptial courtyard serenade. This is the look of the sounds that lull him to sleep.

As with some of the images to follow in the dream sequence proper, as well as the hangover-distorted points of view from the next morning (fig. 22), this shot is far ahead of its time, anticipating the avant-garde experiments of the later 1920s and beyond. Prior to 1924 only a small number of short abstract films had been made. Walter Ruttmann, Hans Richter, Viktor Eggeling, and Oskar Fischinger had experimented with animated geometric forms. At the same time, Bauhaus affiliates Ludwig Hirschfeld-Mack and Kurt Schwerdtfeger had constructed an apparatus halfway between magic lantern and cinema projector that resulted in the interplay of shadows and abstract patterns. None of these works, however, was widely known. (Indeed, Hirschfeld-Mack and Schwerdtfeger's experiments were premiered in the home of Wassily Kandinsky, the artist who claimed to have painted the first abstract picture.[88]) It was not until May 3, 1925, some months after *The Last Laugh*'s premiere, that Ufa sponsored a matinee screening in Berlin of various avant-garde shorts by Ruttmann, Eggeling, Richter, and Hirschfeld-Mack, among others, under the title "The Absolute Film."[89] By "absolute," these filmmakers meant that cinema would be akin to music in its

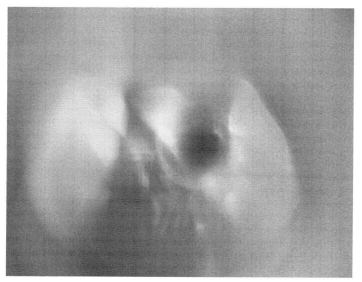

Figure 21. The bell of the horn dissolves into shapes.

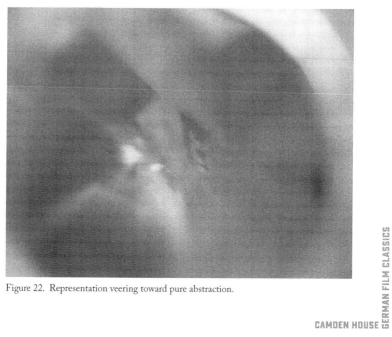

Figure 22. Representation veering toward pure abstraction.

nonrepresentational impetus. To be "absolute," the cinematic work would need to eliminate (or at least minimize) characters, setting, story, and text.

Murnau did not share this aesthetic program. His works are firmly representational and narrative. However, the dream sequence in *The Last Laugh* contains moments of radical experimentation with the dissolution of form that in some respects one-up the programmatic avant-gardists.[90] Ruttmann's and Richter's works rely on the play of clearly identifiable geometric forms. The logic of these films is from the start fully nonrepresentational, and the visual pleasure they offer derives from the fluctuation and movement of lines, shapes, and colors. These may be protean forms, but they make no claim to offer an imitation of our world. Murnau, on the other hand, mobilizes abstraction *within* the representational construct of his film. He demonstrates the dissolution of form, its tendency to distort and lose identifiable shape, as part of a world that we recognize as a copy of our own. Furthermore, Murnau relies solely on the optical affordances of the camera and lens. Ruttmann and Richter use paint and paper, doubly removing their films from reality. What loses form in *The Last Laugh* are the people and things in the pro-filmic frame.[91]

In many ways the dream itself is even more radically experimental than the play with abstraction of the horn-bell shot that precedes it. As we return from that extreme soft-focus image to the close-up of the porter dozing, we see him smile in his sleep before his head is sliced in two by a superimposed image of the hotel's revolving door (fig. 23). This door, however, has been grotesquely stretched to twice its actual height, appearing as a towering rotating column of steel and glass. From inside emerges the uniformed porter, tiny against the huge door. As the real porter's head fades in a dissolve, the camera travels up to his dream-self, now framed in a full shot, proudly saluting. This transition from the porter's dreaming head to his tiny dream-self suggests the doors of his mind have been split open, allowing unfiltered access to his unconscious. His doubling

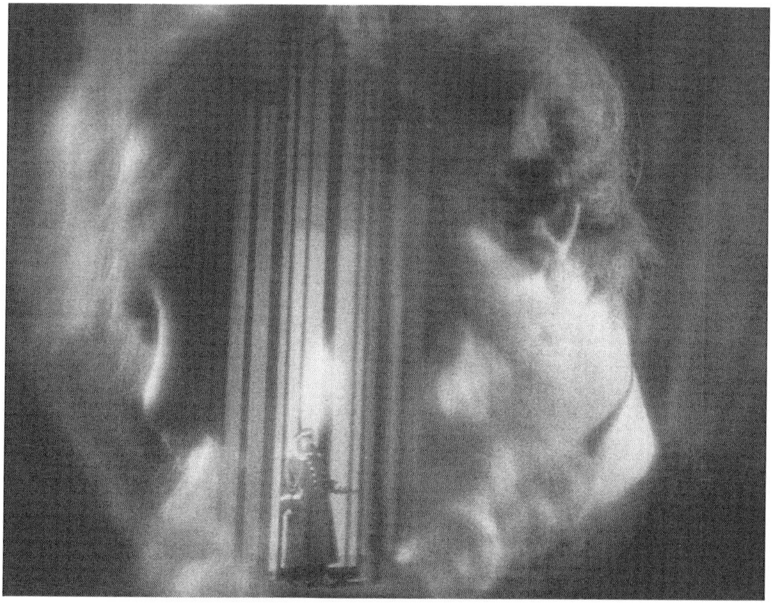

Figure 23. The porter's dream commences with his head being split in two.

anticipates the scene the next morning, when he will encounter his real replacement. Here an imagined version of himself assumes center stage.

The short scene that follows comes the closest of anything in the film—indeed, one might even say closer than in any of Murnau's surviving earlier films—to an Expressionist style. In it, the lighting casts shadows with oblique angles onto a set that would not be out of place in a contemporary film by Robert Wiene or Karl Heinz Martin. The shadows made by the revolving door become part of the play of dark and light, as well. We see a group of bald porters who are unable to lift a trunk from a taxi roof. Jannings's character steps in to help in a comical display of extraordinary physical strength, picking up the trunk easily with one hand (fig. 24). If the dream sequence ended here, it might be seen as merely a nod to an Expressionist

Figure 24. A new Atlas, carrying the legacy of Expressionism.

aesthetic which Murnau seemed to have already mostly abandoned, maybe even as a parody of that style.

But the dream does not end, and where Murnau takes us next ends up looking like little else cinema had previously ventured: in a single take that starts on this side of the revolving door, the viewer crosses into and explores the space beyond. The shot lasts about two and a half minutes. We see Jannings's character carry the trunk through the door, repeatedly toss it high into the air, and catch it again to the applause of those present. Although this single shot adds little to the dream itself, the otherworldly dreamscape it opens is stunning in its uncompromising implementation of a new mode of seeing.

The shot begins after a dissolve from a view of the astonished bald porters. Resembling the distorted horn bell effect from the start of the dream sequence, this dissolve transforms the screen into a

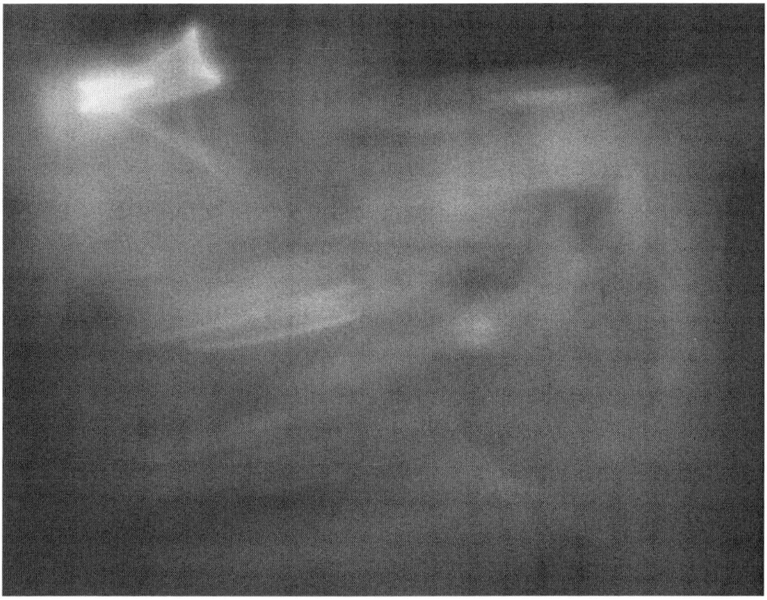

Figure 25. The near-complete dissolution of form in the dream.

web of nearly abstract shapes (fig. 25). The effect appears to have been achieved by adding a filter to the lens, most likely a viscous fluid. From this abstraction Murnau cuts to a blurred close-up of the revolving door, the light smeared across the screen in streaks, a hazy view of people beyond (fig. 26). The two and a half-minute shot that starts here importantly takes us first across this threshold. The crossing itself, so key to the scene of demotion, enters us into a whole new visual world, introducing more moving lines as we pass through the revolving door, its frame and bars continuously sweeping by before also dissolving into abstract shapes (fig. 27). The traveling shot is achieved with a handheld camera that jostles and shakes, making the surroundings blur under low-key lighting, with soft focus and longer exposure time partially doubling the image. As we emerge into the space beyond the door the camera stumbles around, the image bobbing up and down to the cameraman's steps, then passes over the people gathered before taking in the porter's carny-like strongman-cum-Atlas act. The image remains unstable, unfocused, and murky, the motion blur of the slow shutter-speed washing everything in a hazy and indistinct light.

This dream sequence does not exactly provide novel insight into the unconscious. If anything, it relies on an overly facile conception of the dream as wish fulfillment, which Freud says is never expressed directly, but always disguised. The porter's superhuman strength in juggling the travel chest as if it were as light as a balloon would make his dismissal by the hotel manager on the grounds of "decrepitude" laughable. Significantly, however, this display of strength as a consummate fulfillment of his porterly duty is performed not in front of the manager, but moves from a space vaguely reminiscent of the hotel's exterior (the revolving door and a taxi cab are present) to a space that resembles the tenement courtyard, even though it still has features of the lobby, including the elevator. And yet, those present in the dream-lobby, as far as they are recognizable in the shaky and blurred shot, are not his neighbors (with the exception of the horn player who makes an appearance) so much as hotel guests and other employees, such as a group of page boys. These are the people who appreciate his labor. It is them he serves, and it is their appreciation he seeks. When, in the epilogue to the film, Murnau provides another version of this wish fulfillment, presented there as "the author's" fantasy ending, he similarly includes only guests and hotel staff. The old man's family and tenement neighbors are missing from that dream, too.

"The Reality of Things"

The revolving door and the elevator reappear in the porter's dream because they are both key moving parts in the efficient machinery of the hotel that the doorman starts out controlling but ends up being controlled by. Like the elevator, the revolving door reveals

Figure 26. Through the revolving door of the dream.

Figure 27. Play of lines and light anticipating the avant-garde.

an architecture that is dynamic, even agential (recall Kracauer's "whirlpool"). People often find themselves at the mercy of their moving panes, which in their heft can carry you along at an uncomfortable speed or halt and momentarily trap you. These experiences also apply to the elevator, site of entrapment and the fear—exploited in so many movies—of sudden descent or fall. Murnau and Freund's animation of space throughout the film emerges from these already dynamic parts of the building, both of which are introduced in its first shot. At the same time, the viewer is constantly reminded that, though it may appear to be moving on its own, the revolving door requires a person to keep it going. That fact, however, does not so much strip the revolving door of its apparent agency as it integrates the human into the machinery of modern life. The inanimate thing becomes animate, and the animate human at the same time becomes thing-like, a mere part of the apparatus.[92] This dialectic is at work throughout the film.

We see for instance how the porter is treated as an object to be moved as needed, ending up in the washroom less as servant than as a fixture of that space, stuck to the chair as if petrified into a statue. Here he becomes part of a constellation of objects that play various roles in the film. Neither merely props nor ornamental features of the backdrop, inanimate things appear on the one hand "to be infused with a life of their own, with the latent and as yet unknown," as Marc Silberman writes, so that even "the most harmless object seems to conceal fatality."[93] In this manner, objects appear to be "invested with transcendental meaning," as Lotte Eisner puts it, which is to say they serve as symbols.[94] On the other hand, Murnau himself stressed that he was interested in "the reality of things," which suggests something closer to the New Objectivist return to unadorned reality, a desire to let things "speak for themselves."[95] Murnau's caveat to his claim to like "the reality of things, *but not without fantasy*" (emphasis added), refers not to anything fantastical located in these objects but to the affective dimensions of human characters ("reactions and emotions") who interact with them. Murnau names James Joyce as his model, a writer whose preoccupation with the ordinary and usually overlooked objects of everyday life dovetails with his innovative portrayal of consciousness. *The Last Laugh*'s objects do not necessarily assume any of these roles to the exclusion of the others, though usually they index Murnau's newly emerging realist impulses, which include a concern for how the materiality of things can intervene in—and sometimes obstruct—our desires and ambitions.

Indeed, it is the intransigence of things that precipitates the doorman's initial fall. An especially cumbersome travel chest poses a simple problem of transportability that the doorman only overcomes with difficulty. The perverse obstinacy of things (in the German idiom, *die Tücke der Dinge*) lands a blow from which the old man, though not knocked out, will be unable to recover enough to stand on his own again. His dream later drives home how important the real-life struggle with this unruly object is: if he could wield the chest as easily as he does the umbrella, which, as Eisner suggests, functions in his hands as a scepter, balance might be restored and he would be admired and appreciated by all.[96]

Balance seems precisely to be the problem: how do we maintain our grounding in a world seemingly bent on toppling us over? We see this challenge most dramatically when, after receiving his letter of demotion, the porter tries to demonstrate his strength by lifting a nearby trunk. Both he and this unwieldy object end up on the floor. That actual fall has been anticipated in several ways. The downward movement of the opening elevator shot, for instance, traced our protagonist's trajectory to the bowels of the hotel. Then there is the child who falls on the morning of the porter's demotion, ending up in the tenement courtyard dirt (fig. 28). The porter shows her pity in a way none later show him. This child clings to a ragged doll like the doorman clings to his uniform, establishing a relation between anthropomorphic things that infantilizes the old man's obsession with his livery and thereby hints at senility, a proverbial second

Figures 28 and 29. Falling child: foreshadowing the porter's fall (*left*); falling button: lost, overlooked, forgotten object (*right*).

childhood. Another falling object is the lone button that pops off of the porter's uniform during his (literal) defrocking (fig. 29). That button suggests that while he may sneak back and steal the uniform to keep up appearances at home, his status cannot be fully restored. Something has forever been taken from him. Indeed, when the aunt sews on a replacement the next morning, we are reminded of how easy it is to swap out one thing (button or doorman) for another. Once he is stripped of the uniform, an act Eisner refers to as "the equivalent of military degradation," we see him first look down at his unliveried body, as if unable to accept its nakedness.[97] He then sets his sights on the article of clothing that has been taken from him, and which he will later that night steal back. Only then it will serve him as a different kind of costume, a disguise that covers what is missing, hiding how far he has fallen.

The loss associated with the porter being stripped of his uniform finds its ironic reflection and inversion in his daughter's wedding dress, which functions as a female uniform (fig. 30). This gown is the other central article of clothing in the film. Like the porter's uniform, it is shown both on a hanger and on a person and becomes an object that marks a significant shift in social status. Indeed, Jannings's character experiences a double loss the day of his demotion, each connected to the sartorial: the porter taking off his uniform and his daughter

Figures 30 and 31. The uniformed porter eyeing the "female uniform" of the wedding dress (*left*); the loss of paternal status leads to a look of emptiness (*right*).

putting on hers (the ceremonial dress) lead to his loss of social and paternal status, respectively. She may only be moving upstairs, but this move leaves the doorman with an empty nest. His resistance to this otherwise happy occasion is signaled when he inspects the wedding gown, turning to his daughter with a forlorn look and shaking his head. Her response is ambivalent: she seems to comfort him, but also buries her head in his chest, as if she were weeping. The porter looks off screen in this shot with a similarly vacant stare as the one we see on his face after his uniform is taken from him (fig. 31; compare with fig. 33). The association of these two articles of ceremonial clothing is strengthened by way of a crosscut to the wedding march that comes immediately after the porter's uniform is locked away in the hotel manager's closet. The moment at which this livery is fully inaccessible to the old man coincides precisely with the moment in which we see his daughter first wearing her dress.[98]

But the uniform disguises the porter even before he feels compelled to steal it. As a symbol of ceremony and order, it bestows gravity and importance on a man who does not belong to the social class in which, only by virtue of this livery, he maintains a position, however superficial and precarious. Wearing the uniform home uncomfortably conflates worlds that are utterly distinct. The uniform functions in the tenement courtyard and in his apartment as a sign twice removed from its referent. While at the hotel it marks the doorman as head porter, a role that he assumes as if he were a general, his whistle functioning as a military call; in the poor, working-class tenements where he lives the uniform marks him as having the privilege to be employed in the higher class. But his neighbors know where he calls his home. That he assumes these neighbors will respect him commensurately with his estimation of his own importance as doorman precipitates and amplifies the schadenfreude they experience upon his demotion.

Because the porter has mistaken his livery for that which guarantees his importance in the tenement as well as on the job, his demotion is degrading and humiliating. For him, the uniform is more than just work attire; it is a protective shell without which he feels utterly helpless. Jannings's performance stresses the transformation from uniformed porter to defrocked washroom attendant by means of body language. In the former role he stands tall and proud, shoulders back, preening his moustache, saluting the guests, and at one point poised confidently with hands behind his back, looking out across the city as if it were his domain (fig. 32).[99] After losing his uniform, he is hunched over, hair disheveled, hands fumbling for something to hold on to, eyes despondent. He appears lowly, creaturely, vulnerable (fig. 33). The management's verdict of "decrepitude" suddenly rings true, and is further emphasized when the now ex-porter stands catatonically and passively while an assistant to the manager removes his uniform, as if the old man were a feeble patient being undressed in a nursing home.

The reversal of fortunes in this scene codes those involved not just in terms of youth and infirmity, but also in terms of cleanliness and dirtiness. The tenement where the porter lives has already been starkly contrasted with the world of the hotel, the latter's bright, glistening surfaces juxtaposed with the dark and dusty courtyard and stairwell whose concrete walls are coarse and shadowy, dilapidated and in disrepair. Kids play on crumbling brick walls (fig. 34); windows

Figure 32. Body language of the porter: master of his realm.

Figure 33. Defrocked, forlorn: the creaturely porter.

Figures 34 and 35. The dark, dirty, and dilapidated tenement courtyard (*left*); the bright, shimmering hotel lobby (*right*).

are visible half below the ground. Some residents descend into these subterranean quarters to live among the dirt. Later, the porter-as-washroom attendant will work below ground, too, and Murnau shows him eyeing the world above, to which he no longer belongs. His work space now corresponds to the shabby underworld of the lower-class neighborhood. The morning ritual of beating the dust and dirt from rugs indexes the degree to which this world is permeated by uncleanliness.[100] The uniform is among those objects that must be kept pristine. In an early scene, we see the porter's daughter bring it out onto the balcony to brush it clean. When the porter subsequently leaves the apartment for work, the dust clouds sent up from the beating of the rugs—visible in Murnau's careful lighting—have to be fanned and blown away to keep him unblemished.

The hotel manager sees things otherwise. For him, the head porter is sullied. In the demotion scene, when Jannings's character falls trying to demonstrate his ability to lift a trunk, the manager does not even deign to help him up. He instead sends for another porter and then washes his hands, as if he had already gotten too close to the unclean subordinate. As he dries his freshly washed hands, the manager commands the other porter to do the defrocking. The washroom, the space to which Jannings's character is sent after this demotion, is doubly associated with waste and filth.[101] Here the hotel guests remove the dirt and dust from their hands and clothes and relieve themselves of bodily waste before ascending to the immaculate space of the upper floors.

The contrast between these spaces is amplified and ironized by the fact that Jannings's porter sees himself as belonging to the pristine and brilliant opulence of the hotel entrance and lobby (fig. 35). He greatly values his own hygiene and appearance, repeatedly grooming himself and even pulling out a little mirror while working to make sure his ample moustache and muttonchops are properly coiffed. On the morning of his demotion, too, he carefully brushes his hair into place before leaving his apartment. His vanity may be a character flaw; but we are not invited to laugh at or ridicule him. His demotion does not function as a moment of comeuppance: Jannings's porter does not get what he deserves. His fall is tragic and it elicits pathos because he is blindsided by his fate. In classical Greek tragedy, following Aristotle, the reversal of circumstances (peripeteia) often coincides with a recognition (anagnorisis), "a change from ignorance to knowledge" that allows for the hero to see clearly the situation in which he finds himself or the circumstances that have led to it. No such recognition accompanies the porter's fall in *The Last Laugh*. He can only see himself as others do. Murnau demonstrates the New Objectivist credo that the surface is everything: once the porter is stripped of his status-affirming uniform, there is nothing left to see. This invisibility is powerfully dramatized in the encounter with the first washroom guest, who doesn't so much as look at the defeated old man, failing even to recognize his humanity.

The Monstrousness of Shame

The transformation of the porter into a defiled, outcast, and even spectral figure is reflected in the film's mise-en-scène, in particular its lighting. After the demoted porter returns to the tenement, for example, Murnau shows the hunched-over man ascending the stairs

Figure 36. The demoted porter's shadow-self creeps up the stairs.

in a way that recalls a similar ascent by the vampire Nosferatu in his film from two years earlier. In each case we see the shadow of the figure moving slowly up a stairwell wall (figs. 36 and 37). Nosferatu remains all shadow in his approach, sliding, sloping, and stretching his umbral form to enter Ellen's room. Jannings's porter trails behind his shadow, but he is no less a monster. This shot contrasts with a nearly identical one showing the porter's appearance and gradual ascent in front of the same stairwell wall earlier in the film, before his demotion, in which he casts no shadow. Similarly, before his humiliation, the doorman enters the tenement courtyard as a shadowless figure, but after his degradation and transformation, he creeps home and appears in the courtyard in elongated and distorted umbral shapes (figs. 38 and 39).

Figure 37. Shadow of the titular undead monster in *Nosferatu* (1922).

Figures 38 and 39. The warped, ghostly apparitions of the ex-porter.

In each case, he has been reduced to a mere shadow of himself. Before his first return home, he stealthily slides through the halls of the hotel, a man on the prowl, resembling another icon of Expressionist cinema, the somnambulist Cesare played by Conrad Veidt in *The Cabinet of Dr. Caligari* (1920), who similarly slithers through the shadowy streets (figs. 40 and 41). The way the former head porter makes his way through these empty halls, eluding the night watchman's light, recalls numerous scenes that unfold in haunted interior spaces of Expressionist films, from Wiene's defining feature to Murnau's own creepier offerings. Without his disguise, the fallen porter is not just a shadow-self, but is indeed monstrous, eliciting a veritable scream of terror from the aunt when, arriving for a surprise visit, she sees him peeking out from the basement washroom. This scene could just as well be out of a horror film, in which the reveal of the terrifying creature triggers a female scream and a hasty retreat.[102] In the shot of the aunt's banshee-like shriek, Murnau uses the moving camera to swoop in rather than to pull away as he had with the horn player. This scene starts with a shot of the washroom door opening gradually, the porter's face in close-up slowly emerging into view. With a cut to the aunt's reaction, the next shot begins in a medium-close framing from the other side of the glass door and then swiftly travels in to a tight close-up, her breath visible on the glass (fig. 42). The sudden sweep of this shot conveys the porter's subjective experience of seeing her and his quickly intensifying fear.

Indeed, the subsequent shot of Jannings shows him being knocked back by her scream, as if her outburst had physical force. This reaction shot starts with a similar tight close-up of his face, out of focus, before showing him stumbling back, first in horror, then in shame (fig. 43).[103] Who, the viewer will end up asking, is the monster here? The way Murnau's travelling close-up emphasizes the aunt's piercing eyes, her scream, and her ornate and obtrusive black feathered hat positions her as a kind of harpy. As she flees the scene, we see her take off down the hall, away from the hotel, and then running into

Figure 40. The ex-porter haunting the halls of the hotel.

Figure 41. Cesare haunting the village in *The Cabinet of Dr. Caligari* (1920).

Figure 42. The aunt's scream of horror upon seeing the porter without his uniform.

Figure 43. The porter-turned-washroom attendant's terrified reaction to the aunt.

Figures 44 and 45. The aunt as harpy takes flight.

the tenement courtyard and up the stairs, arms outstretched, black cloak flapping behind her as if in flight (figs. 44 and 45).[104]

The aunt's reaction may begin with horror but it ends in mortified contempt. The former porter's family, much like Gregor Samsa's in Kafka's "The Metamorphosis," is not afraid of him so much as ashamed of what he has become, which they find repulsive. As Paul Dobryden puts it, they "treat him as a contaminant."[105] Their reaction may seem overly harsh, especially since the young woman with whom he lives is his daughter, not his niece, as she is often referred to in the film's reception. They express no sympathy for his plight and seem more concerned about themselves being the objects of ridicule. Perhaps they see his demotion only as a ruse perpetrated by someone who, they now suspect, may never have had this position of prominence in the first place. The shocking revelation the aunt brings home is not that Jannings's character has lost his job and importance, but rather that he has been pretending to have this job. Certainly the neighbors' resentment, which quickly transforms into grotesque schadenfreude, rings truer in such a context. From their perspective he has been lording his status over them and has been revealed to be an utter fraud.

The viewer knows better, of course, which lends the film its distinctive pathos. Indeed, the audience is invited to identify and empathize with him. Jannings's character is no hero in the classical sense, however.[106] For one, he lacks a tragic flaw. His shortcomings include a small dose of vanity and a blindness to the fact that the realm over which he stands guard does not actually include him. But neither of these foibles precipitates his fall, which is the consequence of little more than his aging and therefore his inability to carry a traveling chest from taxi to lobby without taking a brief rest to recover from the exertion. His decline is a natural one; his response one of shame, not guilt. Stealing the uniform to hide the truth is his only real transgression, which is motivated by an understandable fear of ridicule and a noble desire to avoid ruining his daughter's wedding with the bad news of his demotion.

Yet if we read the porter's trajectory allegorically as a representation of the declining German Empire it becomes difficult to remain sympathetic. For this reason, most critics are unwilling to separate their judgment of this character from their judgment of what he supposedly represents. Siegfried Kracauer suggests that the uniformed porter embodies "supreme authority" and that the film "advances … the authoritarian credo that the magic spell of authority protects society from decomposition." The viewer may not be compelled to assume the position of the gossiping housewives, whose resentment at being "socially abandoned and thrown back into the gloominess of their flats and of their souls" emerges from their "evil lower middle-class instincts," but the porter's self-pity still invites little sympathy.[107] Most subsequent readers of the film render a similar verdict.[108] Sabine Hake, for example, locates the "attitudes and behaviors" that "reflect the authoritarian, militaristic, and hierarchically structured society of the Wilhelmine Empire" in Jannings's character, describing him as "paternalistic, misogynistic, and authoritarian."[109] Hake argues that although he may at times appear sympathetic or harmless, he nonetheless personifies the "particular national physiognomy, social type, and historical consciousness" of "the authoritarian past," displaying all the "smugness and pretension" as well as "servility and self-pity" of the authoritarian personality.[110]

Such a figure becomes an ambivalent object of identification, because although he is presented as a victim, he stands for a regressive, leftover element of the Wilhelmine era that "must be expelled from the modern designs for living" so that "more democratic structures and egalitarian principles" might thrive. For Hake, then, the porter provokes "equally strong feelings of compassion and contempt," "sympathy as well as mockery."[111]

As convincing as allegorical readings such as Hake's may be, they do not at all describe the character of the porter, whom Jannings plays in a manner that simply does not invite this level of disdain. The elderly doorman in fact displays numerous virtues. We see his love for his daughter, his compassion for the young girl who falls, his generosity in giving her sweets, and his genuine love for his job, which involves helping strangers. He takes visible joy in selflessly serving others. The vanity he exhibits does not harm anyone except, ultimately, himself. The ostentatious display of self-assuredness with which he greets his own neighbors does not come across as arrogant.[112] Nor do others perceive him in this way. They are shown responding kindly to him with genuine neighborly goodwill. Whatever amusement they get from his manner and appearance is benign. Only once they think he has been duping them do they turn on him. The sole failing of this otherwise compassionate and caring individual, then, is his inability to see that his value as a human being does not depend on appearance and the supposed status it confers.

This presentation of a benevolent elderly man is, however, complicated by the doorman's performance of masculinity. His proud, preening stance (fig. 32) and incessant saluting project an image of the self-satisfied and superior male, a display exacerbated by its association with militarism and authoritarianism. On the one hand, it is clear that the porter identifies as a strong, able-bodied male and that his inability to lift heavy luggage precipitates a crisis of masculinity.[113] And yet, on the other hand, the loss of his uniform, often read as a castration, really only denies him the *appearance* of authority and strength, neither of which he truly wields in the first place.[114] Moreover, the porter's affectations of conventional masculinity alternate with stereotypically feminine gestures and concerns, as when he primps his hair in front of the mirror (the use of the pocket mirror, in particular, is highly gendered).[115] Further complicating this picture, the porter does not bring his strutting demeanor home to his daughter, with whom he is gentle, even sheepish, the opposite of the overbearing and often violent father who appears in so many films of the period.[116] Ultimately, as is often the case in Murnau's films, gender identification becomes highly ambiguous in *The Last Laugh*, especially, as we will see, in the epilogue.[117]

In the end, as the site of different and conflicting sociocultural codes that do not always align with expected behavior, the dishonored porter remains difficult to pin down. How then are we supposed to respond to this figure? Do we sympathize with his fate or reject what he appears to stand for? Can we do both? A closer look at the way Murnau ends the film will help answer these critical questions.

The Doubled Ending

The Last Laugh has two endings. One follows the other, after the only title of the film that breaks the hitherto uninterrupted flow of images.[118] The text that appears on the screen at around the hour and a quarter mark tells us that what follows picks up the story of the doorman from where we last saw him. Viewers are thus supposed to understand the turn of events presented in the subsequent epilogue, which takes up between 15 and 20 percent of the entire feature, as a continuation of the ex-porter's story. Nonetheless, another reading is suggested by the tone of the "author's" note that introduces this finale:

> Here, at the place of his humiliation, the old man would waste away miserably for the rest of his life, and here the story would actually be over. But the author is looking

out for him who has been abandoned by everyone, and so he bestows upon him an epilogue, telling a story that—unfortunately—usually doesn't occur in real life.

This authorial intervention breaks the realistic illusion of the film in a remarkable way. It plainly admits that what we are seeing is invention and indeed that the events of the story follow the whims of the "author," figured as an omniscient being who can pity his own creations and give them what he feels they deserve.[119] And yet, precisely for this reason, the epilogue that follows does not undo the story's first and "actual" ending. It, too, may be invention, but it is much closer to reality than the wish fulfillment the author grants his lowly protagonist. As a result, the second ending's highly affirmative turn of events only draws attention to the first, not as a fate that was avoided, but rather as a more plausible—in other words, more realistic—end to the porter's tale. By foregrounding the second ending as a *deus ex machina* that allows the creator to intervene in his tale and bring it to a happy close, Murnau's metafictional interruption achieves something paradoxical. It affirms the first ending—along with everything that has happened in the film up to this point—as a representation grounded in the principle of verisimilitude, a story that corresponds to the real world in which its viewers live, the one they will return to after the lights come up and they exit the theater.[120]

If the first ending is the more faithful picture of contemporary Germany, especially before the stabilization of 1924, then it cannot be erased by the fairy tale that follows. Instead of continuing the porter's story, then, and somehow bringing it to a more desirable close, the epilogue functions as an alternative ending, offering the viewer another way things might have turned out—however unlikely. And the emphasis remains on that unlikelihood. Before examining this second ending in detail, let us look at how the main story of the film comes to its first, heartbreaking end and why that end still haunts the epilogue's fantasy of luck and fulfillment.

The first closing sequence begins after the aunt's revelation has made the rounds at the tenement. We first see the old man emerge from the hotel washroom, fully defeated. He exits not through the main revolving door, which seems no longer to be available to him, but through a side door leading straight into the hotel's subterranean realm. The camera, facing but moving with him, travels backwards as he traipses through the crowd in front of the hotel (careful viewers will see the wheel tracks from the primitive dolly on the street). A subsequent shot contrasts this retreat with a dolly up to the revolving door, helmed by the new porter. After picking up the stolen uniform from the train station, the doorman arrives at his tenement, expecting to be able to continue his deception. Instead, he is greeted with collective mockery and cruel laughter. Murnau films the ex-porter's walk of shame through the courtyard with a backward movement of the camera resembling his retreat from the hotel, except that here it is not on a wheeled platform. Freund's handheld camera moves unsteadily, lumbering in front of Jannings as the latter is bombarded with cries from the gossiping women. The camera then picks up pace with the humiliated man as he tries to escape their ridicule. And while the ex-porter manages to flee offscreen to the right, he cannot fully evade their scorn, which is shown to overpower him in a superimposed collage of shrieking faces, a grotesque, misogynistic display of female derision (fig. 46).[121]

In the scene that follows, the ex-doorman's family rejects him, too. This rather extreme turn of events may seem incredible to modern viewers. But recall the climate of this period in the Weimar Republic, where socioeconomic circumstances had destroyed so much, leaving a country in which every person fought for him- or herself, blamed the next person for the struggles shared by all, therefore leaving "precious little empathy for others."[122] Robert Schechtman argues that *The Last Laugh* depicts "a crisis of community" that extends well beyond the "autonomized, globalized urban space" into the fallen porter's private sphere: "the film's ultimate tragedy occurs within the

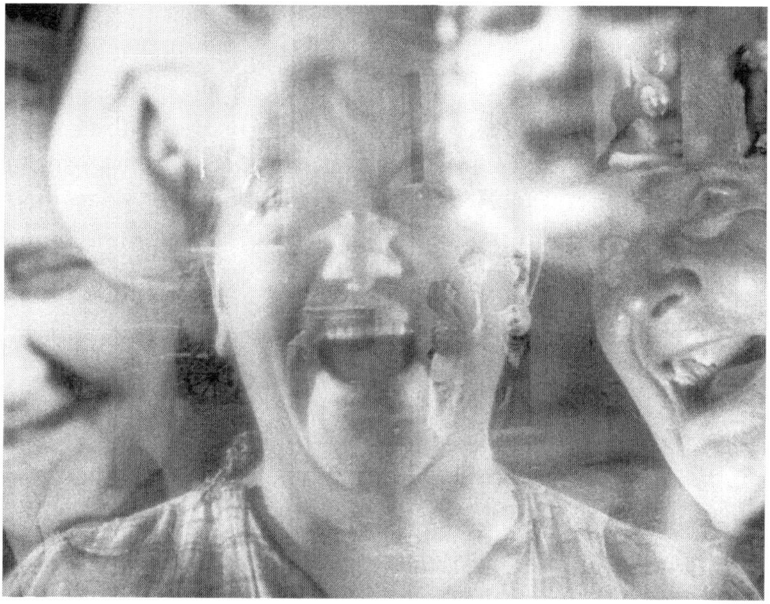

Figure 46. The faces of mockery; laughter as humiliating assault.

man's own community."[123] Does his own daughter reject him? The difficulty of reconciling her behavior with that of an actual daughter may account for why she is so often wrongly referred to in the film's reception as his niece. But Maly Delschaft's character is in fact the only one who weeps at her father's fate. Her expressions of concern are reined in by her new husband and his aunt, who display nothing but contempt. The aunt's response of laughter, however, is clearly contrasted with the daughter's tears.

Nonetheless, the daughter chooses her new family over her old one, so that in the end the old man has no choice but to return to his second home, the hotel. Here the rejected porter encounters the only person who not only displays but also importantly acts upon his sympathy: the night watchman. In the final sequence before the break to the epilogue, this other lowly hotel worker bonds with

Jannings's defeated washroom attendant. The night watchman is played by the marvelous Georg John, known for his roles in films by Fritz Lang, among others (including two previous Murnau pictures). John would become iconic as the blind balloon salesman in Lang's 1931 masterpiece *M*. Here, by contrast, he makes vision possible, the portable lamp about his neck serving as a guiding light through the dark halls of the hotel. The night watchman assures the return of the stolen uniform to its proper place in the manager's closet and also the return of the ex-porter himself to his proper place in the bowels of the hotel, the quavering and bobbing circular light of his lamp pointing the way.

But Georg John's character does not aid the demoralized and helpless ex-porter so much as provide him comfort in this moment of complete humiliation and weakness. Kenneth S. Calhoon reads the final scene in the washroom as a *pietà*, the watchman's lamp casting a halo on the abject and doubly defrocked old man (Jannings is wearing neither his porter's uniform nor the white livery of the washroom attendant), who is hunched over on the chair (fig. 47). The watchman bends over him in a gesture of true compassion, "as if to hear a dying confession," recalling the Christian iconography in which an empathic figure "confers dignity upon the meek and downtrodden" (the *pietà* originally depicted Mary cradling the dead Jesus).[124] The future trajectories of these two actors, however, cast an ironic and tragic light on this image. John, whom the Nazis later classified a "full-blooded Jew" (*Volljude*), would die in the Łódź ghetto in 1941, while Jannings, named "Artist of the State" by the Nazi's Minister of Propaganda Josef Goebbels, continued to star in numerous prestige productions of the Third Reich.

Calhoon also rightly connects this ending to its echo in Josef von Sternberg's *Der blaue Engel* (The Blue Angel) from 1930, in which Jannings plays the humiliated Professor Rath, discovered in the final shot clinging to his teacher's desk, a night watchman's lamp illuminating his head in the dark (fig. 48). Although these men

Figure 47. The first, "actual" ending: a *pietà*—complete with halo.

Figure 48. Jannings in the final shot of *The Blue Angel* (1930).

arrive at their nadirs differently, they both have been led astray in some fashion, which Calhoon links to the Romantic motif of the will-o'-the-wisp, in German *Irrlicht* (a "wandering light," but also with the suggestion of being misled), here made visible in the round, roaming spotlight of the watchman's lamp.[125] This instance of diegetic lighting, in which the source of illumination is explicitly shown to be coming from within the filmic world, demonstrates a feature that Thomas Elsaesser has associated with Murnau's idiosyncratic style: objects are not only lit (extradiegetically) but also become the source of light within the world of the film (diegetically). Elsaesser carries over this notion of illumination to the cinematic image as such, which becomes "an object endowed with a special luminosity (being lit and at the same time radiating light)" that "appears as both cause and effect, active and passive." The result is that, projected on the screen, "the object, and the human actor as object become irreducibly immanent, more-than-real in their 'there-ness' and 'now-ness,'" such that "the luminous becomes ominous becomes numinous."[126]

This use of specifically diegetic lighting draws attention to the affordances of extradiegetic lighting, the ways in which a film's verisimilitude is only made possible by means of a complex artifice of light and shadow coming from off-screen sources. The night watchman's lamp foregrounds the lighting that is usually elided in the mise-en-scène, reminding us at once of the stage spotlights that are not needed in the cinema and of the fact that cinematic ambience (of which Murnau was a master)—the "numinous" to which Elsaesser refers—is most effectively achieved when the source of lighting remains ambiguous. That illumination in this scene should come from a lamp that the night watchman holds against his chest (and in one shot also from the match he uses to light his pipe [fig. 49]) therefore takes on metacinematic value, not only hinting at the very artifices by which a film is properly lit, but also, in the context of this film's innovations in camera movement, evoking the picture of Karl Freund on set with the apparatus strapped to his body (fig. 16).[127]

Figure 49. Doubled illumination coming from the objects within the diegetic space: the night watchman with lamp and lit match.

But the night watchman's lamp also carries symbolic value that encourages and reinforces an empathetic view of the porter's predicament. Indeed, the lighting in this final shot takes on redemptive qualities that numinously transfigure the lowly and defeated man's suffering, making it meaningful as an endpoint to his story, certainly more meaningful than in the epilogue that follows. Murnau's mise-en-scène importantly acknowledges the fallen porter's plight not only as real but also as deserving of compassion, which is modeled for the audience as a proper and necessary response to his tragic trajectory.

The epilogue, which I am calling an "alternative ending," shifts tone so dramatically that we would be forgiven for thinking another director had taken over. Here we encounter a level of excess and joviality that we might find in a contemporaneous comedy by Ernst Lubitsch. Indeed, the images that introduce this new ending present to us models of mirth, faces whose emotional expressions tell us, as viewers, how we should respond before we even know what is so funny. We first see a group of hotel guests seated in the lobby, bowled over with laughter at something they have read in the newspaper. This wide shot is followed by a swift sequence of ten medium close-ups of these and other guests and employees, all laughing with newspaper in hand. Murnau brings us back to the initial wide shot before letting us see what it is in the newspaper that has triggered this outburst of hilarity.

The text of the paper relates the felicitous turn of events intimated in the intertitle. We learn that the once humiliated porter has inherited an "immeasurably vast fortune" from a Mexican multimillionaire who passed away suddenly in the hotel washroom and who had stipulated in his will that his entire estate would go to the person in whose arms he dies. What the article calls "a sensational inheritance" becomes a "sensational" story for the papers—and functions equally as a "sensational" twist in the ex-porter's tale. As such, it seems highly contrived. That the filmmaker has essentially admitted as much in the preceding title card seems almost unnecessary once we come upon the name of the deceased multimillionaire: A. G. Money. The pun of this name—A. G. stands for "Aktiengesellschaft," meaning "corporation" and the surname in English would have been legible to all Germans—is so obvious as to only heighten the unreality of the occurrence.[128]

As important as this newspaper story is, Murnau seems far more interested in the response to it, intercutting a shot of one part of the story with the same gaggle of laughing hotel guests we saw at the start of the sequence and following the second shot of the printed text with a long, gliding take that moves us through the hotel restaurant, where we see the paper being passed from table to table, bringing laughter in its wake.

Murnau clearly wishes to juxtapose this manifestation of laugh-ter with the monstrous mocking of the tenement women. Both represent collective responses to "news" about the ex-porter that we see quickly spreading among the public. And in each case the response appears exaggerated, even grotesque, an expression of emotion not commensurate with the content of the respective piece of news. Moreover, in each case, the original source of the news comes from the washroom. In the first ending, however, this lavatory represented the subterranean realm from which a dirty secret had emerged, whereas in the second ending it becomes a space of joyful coincidence and transformation—a place not of impurity but of ablution and renewal.

So what is there to laugh about? The English title of the film cleverly picks up the idiom "to have the last laugh," indicating, as *Merriam-Webster* puts it, "the satisfaction of ultimate triumph or success especially after being scorned or regarded as a failure." This definition seems to encapsulate the ex-porter's fate in the reimagined ending, in which he has indeed fully overcome his predicament, having found fortune and friendship in spite of his earlier debasement and rejection. However, the idiom alluded to in the English title is somewhat misleading. To begin with, the now-rich ex-porter is not the one laughing. In fact, the "satisfaction" he displays is not that of having "triumphed" over anyone. Of those who had scorned him, only the hotel manager is present, and Jannings's character does not treat him with derision or resentment. Most importantly, though, using this idiom as the title places the emphasis of the entire film firmly on the second ending, as if this were the culmination and proper close to the story. The original German title, *Der letzte Mann*—"The Last Man"—unequivocally points to the first ending.

But even if the "last laugh" depicted in the epilogue were meant to be taken as the final word on the fate of the old doorman, it remains ambiguous. It may be that the ex-doorman gets the proverbial last laugh. This sequence, however, leaves the strong impression that the laughter of the hotel guests and employees is not a spontaneous eruption of joy at his newfound fortune, but rather that the laughter is at his expense. Seen thus, he remains the object of contempt; only now it is his fortune, not his misfortune, that provokes this response. In any event, the excessive laughter at the start of this final sequence casts a further shadow on the former porter's already dubious luck. Whatever realism the film had established up to this epilogue crumbles as we witness a gratuitous display of mirth that might best be read as a response to the implausibility of the old man's fate and thus to the absurdity of this contrived ending as a last-ditch effort by the filmmaker to rescue his protagonist.

The gratuitous display does not end with the laughter, however. It carries over to the decadent dining ritual that then unfolds as we witness Jannings's character indulge in what Marc Silberman aptly describes as an "eating orgy," gleefully attacking an immense banquet of culinary delights, which are wheeled up to his table in a seemingly endless supply, even requiring a trio of chefs nearby and a whole army of attending waiters.[129] But the porter-turned-gourmand does not gormandize alone. He is soon joined by his friend, the night watchman, who is fully discombobulated as he enters the dining hall laden with boxes from a shopping spree. The ex-porter's joy, importantly, is not a self-centered indulgence but a joint satisfaction shared with the one person who showed him pity. If we side even in part with those who find fault in the old man, we must remain excluded from this celebration, banished perhaps to the peripheral onlookers who can only uncomfortably laugh. If we sympathize with him, this moment of friendship offers up the only solace in the film, even if it comes in the form of a fairy-tale—and thus false—ending.

In allegorical readings, this ending brings the film right up to the time of its making. Germany's military and economic decline has reached bottom; the way forward is only possible with the help of foreign "Money." From this very contemporary perspective, the fortune the disgraced porter inherits from the "Mexican" multimillionaire stands in for the Dawes Plan, the agreement struck in August of 1924—right in the middle of the film's production—

that brought an end to Germany's hyperinflation by means of a huge influx of American capital. This may be an enticing interpretation, though it leads to a reading of Jannings's character that is irreconcilable with his sympathetic portrayal, one that requires us to welcome his downfall as we would that of the old Wilhelmine values standing in the way of modern progress. Such a response would align us with the tenement women and the people in the hotel, contemptuously jeering at the old man's fate. The reason so many critics feel obliged to take this stance is that the alternative would seem to put them in a morally—and politically—questionable position. For in taking pity on the disgraced doorman, are we not embracing the old, authoritarian world of the Empire, lamenting its disappearance, and thereby joining the reactionaries whose resentment would feed into the fascist takeover of Germany eight years later?[130]

This ethical bind, however, presents itself only if we regard the porter as a stand-in for the Wilhelmine Empire, with which he ultimately has nothing in common besides his superficial appearance. As "a parable about the difference between identity and false image," the film itself is constantly reminding us that the value we invest in appearances is illusory.[131] The porter's uniform does not of course make him an aristocrat or a military man. A contemporary poster shows the uniform being taken from him by blue hands, which represent the "blue-blooded" nobility reclaiming what does not belong to the ex-porter (fig. 50). He is firmly aligned with the lower class, those "locked out" from the privileged world of the elite.[132] What is sad about his story is not that by losing his uniform he loses his worth, but that this loss reveals that his own sense of worth only comes from the precarious and chimerical status this symbol seems to grant him. In recognizing that his worth does not depend on these superficial trappings, we also recognize the virtues (kindness, generosity, empathy, paternal love) of which it is actually comprised.

Murnau's film, however, cannot be separated from its historical context, and it would be a mistake to claim that Jannings's character

Figure 50. Lithograph by Theo Matejko (used for the original film poster) depicting a "blue-blooded" class recovering its status symbol. Source: La Cinémathèque française.

has nothing to do with Germany. Rather than identifying him as the embodiment of regressive Wilhelmine values, we might instead read him and his experience as reflecting back the contradictions and struggles of the contemporary Weimar Republic.[133] In this way, the film's dramatic impact and its ethical stance snap into focus. Jannings's porter emerges as the site of conflict and ambiguity, of both old and new values, of confusions and uncertainties, a figure fighting to survive at an unresolved, incomplete moment of transition. In 1924, Germany was an old country seeking a new life, one still clinging to the symbols and ceremonies of the old order while nonetheless thrust into a new, modern world. Not yet fully able to come to terms with this world and its place in it, the country remained precariously on the cusp, still finding its way in the liminal zone between these realms and what they represented.

From this perspective, instead of disdaining the porter, we can and should feel pity for him, and even extend him compassion. Murnau allows the audience to see what the old man cannot: that his worth has nothing to do with his social status or the livery that allows him to hide it. As a result, his struggle becomes palpable and real and, in the end, tragic. And if friends are the only aid to navigating this unpredictable and often unforgiving time at the intersection of old and new (recall the night watchman's guiding light), it is telling that the final scene of the second ending shows a new community of friends—two men and a tramp—riding off not in an automobile but in a horse-drawn carriage, vestige of the former world, firmly implanted in the new one. Where Sabine Hake sees the ex-hotel employees in the epilogue "coyly playing husband and wife," Thomas Elsaesser spies a bona fide "homoerotic scenario, in which the doorman and the night watchman ride off as the perfect couple, with the young beggar boy they have just picked up as their 'son' in tow."[134] That queer family unit, though, is as much a part of Murnau's wish fulfillment as the rest of the alternative ending, offering only a glimmer of (unrealizable) utopian possibility against the backdrop of an otherwise bleak assessment of the unstable transition between Germanies.

Since it has so few title cards to begin with, maybe it is not surprising that the film also lacks a final one indicating that it is over. Is this Murnau's way of indicating that his story is indeed set in the present historical moment and is thus ongoing? Does that make this last part of the film a beginning instead of an ending? Or is this lack of "The End" another means to remind us that the real ending has already come and gone? The final fade-out with Jannings's character waving, the hotel's name prominently behind him, provides no answers, but it does suggest that he—along with the audience of 1924—were crossing over another kind of Atlantic, an uncharted divide between the old world and the new. Little did anyone at the time know that the promise this new world offered would not last long. In fact, just three days prior to *The Last Laugh*'s premiere, Hitler was released from prison and would immediately begin his political comeback, culminating, eight years later, in the end of the Weimar Republic. What Murnau presents as a conflicted transitional moment turns out, in hindsight, to be an all-too-brief interlude between empire and dictatorship.

CREDITS

Director:
Friedrich Wilhelm Murnau

Scenario:
Carl Mayer

Distribution:
Universum Film A.G. (Ufa)

Produced by:
Erich Pommer

Cast:
Emil Jannings (porter)
Maly Delschaft (daughter)
Max Hiller (groom)
Emilie Kurtz (groom's aunt)
Hans Unterkircher (hotel manager)
Georg John (night watchman)
Olaf Storm (young guest)
Hermann Vallentin (potbellied guest)
Emmy Wyda (thin neighbor)

Music:
Giuseppe Becce (at premiere)

Cinematography:
Karl Freund
Robert Baberske (assistant)

Set Design:
Robert Herlth
Walter Röhrig
Edgar G. Ulmer (assistant)

Costume Design:
G. Benedict (uniform)

Film Length:
2315 meters (premiere)
2018 meters (2001/2002 restoration)

Runtime:
101 minutes (premiere, at 20fps)
88 minutes (2001/2002 restoration,
    at 20fps)

Release Date:
December 23, 1924 (premiere at
    Ufa-Palast am Zoo, Berlin)

Cameras:
Debrie Parvo L
Stachow Filmer

Cinematographic Process:
Spherical

Printed Film Format:
35mm

Color:
Black and white (no tinting)

Locations:
Shot between late May and late
    September 1924 at the Ufa-Atelier
    Berlin-Tempelhof and Ufa-Freigelände
    Neubabelsberg (today Studio
    Babelsberg)

NOTES

1   Haas takes the language here from Goethe's remark about the French Revolution ("from here on out begins a new epoch in the history of the world"). Willy Haas, "Der letzte Mann," *Film-Kurier* 303, December 24, 1925: 1. Unless otherwise indicated, all translations here and throughout are my own.

2   *Die Filmwoche* 2, January 13, 1925.

3   Andrew Sarris, *The American Cinema: Directors and Directions 1929–1968* (New York: E. P. Dutton, 1968), 69.

4   Murnau's earlier 1924 feature, *Die Finanzen des Großherzogs* (The Finances of the Grand Duke), his only comedy, marks his first step in this direction, though its high-jinx adventure plot sets it apart from the sober realism of *The Last Laugh*. Jameux draws attention to the "paradox" that for the fantastical elements of *Nosferatu* (1922) Murnau used exterior locations and natural décor, whereas he achieved the everyday reality of *The Last Laugh* entirely in a studio and with elaborate sets. Charles Jameux, *F. W. Murnau* (Paris: Éditions universitaires, 1965), 12.

5   Lotte H. Eisner, *The Haunted Screen: Expressionism in the German Cinema and the Influence of Max Reinhardt*, revised edition, trans. Roger Greaves (Berkeley and Los Angeles: University of California Press, 1973), 97. This book was first published in 1952 as *L'Ecran démoniaque*.

6   Thomas Elsaesser writes that of the Weimar-era filmmakers, Murnau "has always seemed the most enigmatic, though probably the one best loved by film makers and cinephiles." Thomas Elsaesser, *Weimar Cinema and After: Germany's Historical Imaginary* (London and New York: Routledge, 2000), 223.

7   Elsaesser, *Weimar Cinema and After*, 224.

8   "If his films carry some special secret message (about Murnau the man) in the narratives, it is unlikely to be about a love that dare not speak its name, but rather of passions that find fulfillment in distance and contemplation, sometimes of an idealized self-image." Elsaesser, *Weimar Cinema and After*, 249.

9   Elsaesser, *Weimar Cinema and After*, 224. Eight of Murnau's pre-*Last Laugh* pictures have been partly or completely lost.

10   The tactic of using "Nosferatu" in place of "Dracula" did not prevent the Stoker estate from winning a later lawsuit, which bankrupted Prana, the production company of Murnau's film.

11   Lubitsch, Wilder, and Ulmer also ended their careers in Hollywood. Although all of the films Lang directed between 1936 and 1957 were made in Hollywood, for his last two films he returned to Europe.

12   Quoted in Lotte H. Eisner, *Murnau*, revised edition (Berkeley and Los Angeles: University of California Press, 1973), 67. First published in French in 1964.

13 "Best Unique and Artistic Picture" was only awarded at the first Academy Awards, where it was a category on par with but distinct from "Outstanding Picture" (today, "Best Picture").

14 *4 Devils*, which was shot as a silent picture and premiered October 1928 in this form, was rereleased in June 1929 in a talkie version, though the dialogue sequences, in which Murnau was not involved, were only added at the end of the film. *City Girl* (1930), although intended and shot as a silent picture, was refitted with talk sequences for the premiere, though not until after Murnau had already left Fox. Although *4 Devils* remains lost, the silent version of *City Girl* was found in the Fox vaults in 1970. Murnau did not completely oppose the talkie, which he said "represents a great step forward in the cinema." He did, however, feel that it had "come too soon: we had just begun to find our way with the silent film and were beginning to exploit all the possibilities of the camera. And now here are the talkies and the camera is forgotten while people rack their brains about how to use the microphone." Quoted in Eisner, *Murnau*, 213–14.

15 Claudia Heydolph notes that no mention of this first title card is made in contemporary reviews and discussions of the film. Claudia Heydolph, *Der Blick auf das lebende Bild: F. W. Murnaus "Der letzte Mann" und die Herkunft der Bilderzählung* (Kiel: Ludwig, 2004), 68. Murnau himself says that "*The Last Laugh* had only one [intertitle]," which makes clear that he conceived of this first title card as part of the opening credits. Murnau's own thoughts on the titleless feature are summed up in the title of the article from which this quotation is taken: Friedrich Wilhelm Murnau, "The Ideal Picture Needs No Titles: By Its Very Nature the Art of the Screen Should Tell Its Story Pictorially," *Theatre Magazine*, January 1928: 41. In a response to a query from the magazine *Film-Kurier* in 1924 about his "ideal screenplay," Murnau says that while the title card, which he defines as "something that logically comes between images," may be "unavoidable at first," it is "quite simply an obstructive presence in film." Fritz Lang and F. W. Murnau, "My Ideal Screenplay," in *The Promise of Cinema: German Film Theory 1907–1933*, ed. Anton Kaes, Nicholas Baer, and Michael Cowan (Oakland, CA: University of California Press, 2016), 499.

16 Patrick Vonderau writes that the titleless film was associated with Murnau because he was the first to have "perfected" it. Patrick Vonderau, "27 May 1921: *Scherben* Seeks Cinematic Equivalent of Theatrical Intimacy," in *A New History of German Cinema*, ed. Jennifer M. Kapczynski and Michael D. Richardson (Rochester, NY: Camden House, 2012), 108. For an excellent detailed discussion of the contemporary debates about the titleless film, see Anjeana K. Hans, *Warning Shadows* (Rochester, NY: Camden House, 2021), 14–23.

17 Originally published in *Der Montag* 49 (December 22, 1924). This was written after the "trade show" premiere in New York City on December 5, 1924, which probably featured a slightly different cut of the film.

18 François Truffaut, *Hitchcock*, revised edition (New York: Simon and Schuster, 1985), 31.

19 Donald Spoto, *The Dark Side of Genius: The Life of Alfred Hitchcock* (London: Collins, 1983), 68.

20   Mariann Lewinsky, *Eine verrückte Seite: Stummfilm und filmische Avantgarde in Japan* (Zurich: Chronos, 1997), 149–53. Lewinsky also points to numerous images, situations, effects, and technical features that *A Page of Madness* shares with *The Last Laugh* (171).

21   Luciano Berriatúa and Camille Blot, "Zur Überlieferung der Filme," in *Friedrich Wilhelm Murnau: Ein Melancholiker des Films*, ed. Hans Helmut Prinzler (Berlin: Bertz, 2003), 224.

22   Berriatúa and Blot, "Zur Überlieferung der Filme," 224. A 16mm copy of the film with intertitles was discovered in 1979. The titles were published in *Die Information*, vols. 1–3 (Wiesbaden: Deutsches Institut für Filmkunde, 1979), xvii–xviii. Among Lotte Eisner's documents held at the Cinémathèque française, I found a playbill for the January 5, 1925 Berlin screening of the film that included these same intertitles, grouped by act divisions. It appears they were provided as a kind of guide to the plot, in the same way an opera playbill includes a summary of the main action.

23   This character is often misidentified as the porter's niece. The playbill from the January 5, 1925 screening (see note 22) clearly states she is his daughter. Claudia Heydolph, who inspected the censor card, says she is listed as the daughter there, too. Heydolph, *Der Blick auf das lebende Bild*, 57n72.

24   Detlev Peukert, *The Weimar Republic: The Crisis of Classical Modernity* (New York: Hill and Wang, 1989), 75, 52, 61.

25   Peukert, *The Weimar Republic*, 53.

26   Peukert, *The Weimar Republic*, 64.

27   Eric D. Weitz, *Weimar Germany: Promise and Tragedy*, revised edition (Princeton, NJ: Princeton University Press, 2018), 135.

28   Weitz, *Weimar Germany*, 137.

29   Peukert, *The Weimar Republic*, 76, 64.

30   Weitz, *Weimar Germany*, 140.

31   The film's place between Expressionist *Kammerspielfilm* and New Objectivity has been noted by other critics, e.g., Marc Silberman, *German Cinema: Texts in Context* (Detroit, MI: Wayne State University Press, 1995), 21; and Robert Schechtmann, "23 December 1924: *Der letzte Mann* Explores Limits of Modern Community" in Kapczynski and Richardson, *A New History of German Cinema*, 149. Sabine Hake elaborates how the film displays the "expressionist–New Objectivist divide along generational lines." Sabine Hake, "Who Gets the Last Laugh? Old Age and Generational Change in F. W. Murnau's *The Last Laugh*," in *Weimar Cinema: An Essential Guide to Classic Films of the Era*, ed. Noah Isenberg (New York: Columbia University Press, 2009), 125.

32   Anton Kaes, "Film in der Weimarer Republik: Motor der Moderne," *Geschichte des deutschen Films*, ed. Wolfgang Jacobsen, Anton Kaes, and Hans Helmut Prinzler, 2nd ed. (Stuttgart: Metzler, 1994), 54.

33   Elsaesser, *Weimar Cinema and After*, 230.

34   Kaes, "Film in der Weimarer Republik," 54.

35 Elsaesser rightly identifies the stylistic palette of many of Murnau's early films, especially *Journey into the Night* and *The Haunted Castle*, as indebted to the Scandinavian school and as drawing more on the work of Victor Sjöström and Mauritz Stiller than on any of his German contemporaries. Elsaesser, *Weimar Cinema and After*, 228.

36 Elsaesser, *Weimar Cinema and After*, 234.

37 Kaes deals with *The Last Laugh* in his discussion of the *Kammerspielfilm*. Kaes, "Film in der Weimarer Republik," 56–57. Elsaesser refers to its "realism in detail and décor, and the *Kammerspiel* plot with its self-tormented characters," aligning it with *Hintertreppe*, *Scherben*, and *Sylvester*, all of which are based on Carl Mayer scripts. But he also points to its "Expressionist acting." Elsaesser, *Weimar Cinema and After*, 231. Lotte Eisner notes the overlap of this subgenre with the "Expressionist vision" in Carl Mayer's script: "He was at one and the same time an Expressionist writer and a poet of the *Kammerspiel*." Eisner, *Murnau*, 147.

38 Lupu Pick directed the first two films in the trilogy and was supposed to direct and act in the third. A disagreement with Mayer led to the project coming to Murnau instead. Eisner, *The Haunted Screen*, 207–8.

39 Eisner, *Murnau*, 158. Göttler similarly writes that in his last three German films with Jannings, Murnau "frees himself fully, for Hollywood, from the *Kammerspiel* and its dramatic implications." Fritz Göttler, "Kommentierte Filmografie," in *Friedrich Wilhelm Murnau*, ed. Peter W. Jansen and Wolfram Schütte (Munich: Carl Hanser, 1990), 166.

40 Eisner, *Murnau*, 147.

41 The excerpts from Mayer's script that were published show how heavily indebted he was to the Expressionist tradition. The screenplay makes use of a similar compressed, clipped language and exclamatory urgency that one finds in the Expressionist dramas of Georg Kaiser or Reinhard Goering. See Carl Mayer, "Der letzte Mann," *Das Tagebuch* (1924): 1854–56.

42 Lotte H. Eisner, *Murnau: Der Klassiker des deutschen Films* (Hannover: Friedrich Verlag, 1967), 126.

43 Silberman, *German Cinema*, 19.

44 Silberman, *German Cinema*, 23. Despite these facts and the unanimous praise the film received in Germany and abroad, it was not a success with audiences and was a financial failure. See Heydolph, *Der Blick auf das lebende Bild*, 67n94.

45 On the film's connections to New Objectivity, see Helmut Weihsmann, "Virtuelle Räume: Die Formsprache der Neuen Sachlichkeit bei Friedrich Wilhelm Murnau," in *Die Metaphysik des Dekors: Raum, Architektur und Licht im klassischen deutschen Stummfilm*, ed. Klaus Kreimeier (Marburg: Schüren Presseverlag, 1994), 22–48.

46 Quoted in Eisner, *Murnau: Der Klassiker des deutschen Films*, 127.

47 Frieda Grafe, "Der Mann Murnau: Eine kommentierte Biographie," in Jansen and Schütte, *Friedrich Wilhelm Murnau*, 13.

48   On how the introduction of the elevator into modern buildings reorganized urban space and its socioeconomic values, see Andreas Bernard, *Lifted: A Cultural History of the Elevator* (New York and London: New York University Press, 2014). Bernard points to the way in which the elevator's "fragmentation of the building" into discrete floors "obscures" the spaces between them (57–58). He also details the "reversal of vertical order" brought about by the elevator, which corresponds to social hierarchies. In the 1920s, especially in the grand hotel, the top floors became the sites of luxury and glamor while the bottom floors were meant for those less privileged (65–70).

49   Heydolph, *Der Blick auf das lebende Bild*, 107.

50   Some critics have pointed to the revolving door as a meta-cinematic allusion to the camera without, however, specifying the rotating film reel. See, for instance, Schechtmann, "23 December 1924," 148–49. Hake refers to the door as "a foremost symbol of cinema and modernity." Hake, "Who Gets the Last Laugh?," 129.

51   Quoted in Eisner, *Murnau*, 67.

52   Here and elsewhere I treat the opening shot, which in the surviving prints contains a cut, as the originally uninterrupted take.

53   Elsaesser, *Weimar Cinema and After*, 251.

54   Hans Helmut Prinzler, "In weiter Ferne, so nah!," in *Friedrich Wilhelm Murnau: Ein Melancholiker des Films*, ed. Hans Helmut Prinzler (Berlin: Bertz, 2003), 36.

55   On the generational divide, see Hake, "Who Gets the Last Laugh?."

56   Karl Prümm, "Die bewegliche Kamera im mobilen Raum: *Der letzte Mann* von Friedrich Wilhelm Murnau," in *Diesseits der "Dämonischen Leinwand": Neue Perspektiven auf das späte Weimarer Kino*, ed. Thomas Koebner (Munich: edition text + kritik, 2003), 52.

57   Compare with Paul Dobryden's reading of this scene as rendering "the porter's momentary visual impairment," which he interprets in the context of discourses on hygienic able-bodiedness. Paul Dobryden, *The Hygienic Apparatus: Weimar Cinema and Environmental Disorder* (Evanston, IL: Northwestern University Press, 2022), 123–25.

58   Prümm notes that the "framing effects stress the enclosure and impenetrability of the sphere of power." Prümm, "Die bewegliche Kamera im mobilen Raum," 52.

59   Pier Giorgio Tone, *Friedrich Wilhelm Murnau* (Florence: La Nuova Italia, 1976), 77–79.

60   Eisner, *The Haunted Screen*, 210.

61   The grotesque effect of this juxtaposition is heightened by the fact that, as Stephen Brockmann points out, the washroom is the space of human waste, with which the doorman is not only surrounded, but which he has also effectively become. Stephen Brockmann, *A Critical History of German Film*, second edition (Rochester, NY: Camden House, 2020), 82.

62   In an excerpt from the original screenplay the new porter is described as "seeming almost to be his doppelgänger." Mayer, "Der letzte Mann," 1854. See also Silberman, *German Cinema*, 30.

63   Brockmann, *A Critical History of German Film*, 78.

64   Siegfried Kracauer, *From Caligari to Hitler: A Psychological History of the German Film* (Princeton and Oxford: Princeton University Press, 2019), 103. First published in 1947.

65   I therefore agree with Dobryden, who writes that the care home is "the implied end point of the porter's trajectory." Dobryden, *The Hygienic Apparatus*, 121. But I disagree that this end is inevitable because the ex-porter has no spouse or children, which of course is not entirely true. Whether his daughter would actually care for him after retirement, however, remains at best uncertain.

66   Kracauer, *From Caligari to Hitler*, 73–74.

67   Kracauer does not explicitly connect the whirlpool to the revolving door, but he does describe the latter as in permanent motion, and it is clear it belongs to the images of chaos. Kracauer, *From Caligari to Hitler*, 100. Other discussions of the circular motif at 121 and 186.

68   In the same sequence there is what appears to be a crane shot moving up from a high-angle view of a table, but the effect was achieved by keeping the camera stable while the floor was lowered down.

69   Katharina Loew, *Special Effects and German Silent Film: Techno-Romantic Cinema* (Amsterdam: Amsterdam University Press, 2021), 232.

70   Kracauer points to the complementary roles of the film's mobile camera, its (near) lack of titles, and its attention to objects (which I discuss in a later section): "the freed camera develops an activity entirely consistent with the omission of titles and the promotion of objects." Kracauer, *From Caligari to Hitler*, 105. Note that Freund credits Mayer with the prominence of the mobile camera in *The Last Laugh*. Paul Rotha, *The Film Till Now: A Survey of World Cinema*, revised edition (London: Spring Books, 1967), 716–17.

71   Eisner, *The Haunted Screen*, 70. *The Finances of the Grand Duke*, Murnau's early 1924 feature with Freund at the camera, is notable here. Although it includes some moving shots from a car and from boats, there is also a single short tracking shot that could only have been possible with some kind of wheeled platform. Freund, however, claimed not to have used the mobile camera prior to *The Last Laugh.* It is possible he meant that it was not removed from the tripod prior to *The Last Laugh.*

72   Rotha, *The Film Till Now*, 717.

73   Eisner, *Murnau*, 63. Luciano Berriatúa, *Der letzte Mann—Das "Making of."* Documentary film, 2004.

74   Loew, *Special Effects and German Silent Film*, 231.

75   Mayer's scenario specifically calls for this camera movement: "(As if the apparatus flew in the direction of the porter, at an angle upward / The horn player shown always from a high angle. / Whose notes quasi pictorially ascend [*emporfliegen*])." Quoted in Heydolph, *Der Blick auf das lebende Bild*, 117.

76   Quoted in Eisner, *Murnau*, 65.

77 Both Freund (Rotha, *The Film Till Now*, 716–17) and Baberske (Eisner, *Murnau*, 81) say the film had to be reversed.

78 Compare this shift to Deleuze's distinction between movement-image and time-image. In his discussion of the former, he refers to the opening shot of *The Last Laugh*, writing that "the mobile camera is like a *general equivalent* of all the means of locomotion that it shows or that it makes use of—aeroplane, car, boat, bicycle, foot, metro." Gilles Deleuze, *Cinema 1: The Movement-Image*, trans. Hugh Tomlinson and Barbara Habberjam (Minneapolis: University of Minnesota Press, 2001), 22.

79 Mary Ann Doane, *The Emergence of Cinematic Time: Modernity, Contingency, the Archive* (Cambridge, MA: Harvard University Press, 2002), 22.

80 Although Hitchcock made use of the unchained camera in extraordinary ways throughout his career, the long virtuoso take at the end of *Young and Innocent* (1937) should be highlighted here, because it appears to allude to *The Last Laugh* in its combination of the mobile camera and a hotel setting.

81 Buildings are also central to the aforementioned new possibilities inherent in Freund's camera. Consider a much later film set almost entirely in a hotel, *The Shining* (1980), in which director Stanley Kubrick makes use of the handheld camera to explore architectural space in radical new ways. Together with its creator Garrett Brown, Kubrick implemented a modified version of the Steadicam, a stabilizing device that isolates the apparatus from the cameraman's body to allow for smooth movement, to create "supernaturally smooth" shots that seem to assume the perspective of the building itself in "a hotel's-eye-view." Source of quotations: interview with Garret Brown made by the United States Patent and Trademark Office: https://www.youtube.com/watch?v=YpcP-6nBi5c.

82 Quoted in Eisner, *Murnau*, 84.

83 Walter Ruttmann, "Painting with Time," in Kaes, Baer, and Cowan, *The Promise of Cinema*, 451.

84 Murnau's original German for "sobriety" is "Schlichtheit," not "Sachlichkeit." The basic aesthetic principle is nonetheless very similar. The original is reprinted in Fred Gehler and Ullrich Kasten, *Friedrich Wilhelm Murnau* (Augsburg: AV-Verlag Franz Fischer, 1990), 141. The essay originally appeared in *Die Filmwoche* 1 (1924).

85 Elsaesser speculates that Murnau's "obsession with gliding camera movements and intricate spatial set-ups" may be related to his "perception of the curved space and unbounded vistas" he experienced as a pilot. Elsaesser, *Weimar Cinema and After*, 245.

86 Prümm, "Die bewegliche Kamera im mobilen Raum," 54; Silberman, *German Cinema*, 31.

87 This point-of-view drunkenness was famously copied by Martin Scorsese in *Mean Streets* (1973).

88 This painting would be *Composition V* from 1911, though of course Kandinsky was preceded by others, most notably Hilma af Klint.

89   For details, see Joel Westerdale, "3 May 1925: French and German Avant-Garde Converge at *Der absolute Film*," in Kapczynski and Richardson, *A New History of German Cinema*, 160–65.

90   In this context, it needs to be noted that not all the films screened at the "Absolute Film" matinee were nonrepresentational. The final short shown was Francis Picabia and René Clair's *Entre'acte*, which used unusual camera angles, trick shots, and a disconnected series of short scenes and shots for an absurdist effect.

91   Robert Reinert's 1919 film *Nerven* (Nerves) deserves mention here. Johannes's mental breakdown in the middle of this film uses superimposition and distorted lenses to create a similar discombobulating effect, though it never fully abandons the discernable image of this figure, who—unlike Jannings's character in *The Last Laugh*—always remains the object of the camera's eye, never assuming its subject position.

92   See Silberman, *German Cinema*, 29, who sees Jannings's character as becoming part of the revolving door.

93   Silberman, *German Cinema*, 28.

94   Eisner, *The Haunted Screen*, 211.

95   Murnau, "The Ideal Picture Needs No Titles," 41, 72. Weihsmann, "Virtuelle Räume," 25.

96   Eisner, *The Haunted Screen*, 209.

97   Eisner, *The Haunted Screen*, 209–10. Silberman writes that the uniform "is removed from him like a second skin and brings about a metamorphosis of his personality." Silberman, *German Cinema*, 28. Eisner claims the film "can only be understood in a country where uniform is king, not to say God." Eisner, *The Haunted Screen*, 207. Others refer to the uniform as fetish object, e.g., Tone, *Friedrich Wilhelm Murnau*, 76 and Gehler and Kasten, *Friedrich Wilhelm Murnau*, 74. Hake writes that the uniform "functions like an external armor" but also as a "prosthesis," and that it is, generally, "the founding site of male identity" that "reveals the porter as product of prewar militarism and authoritarianism." Hake, "Who Gets the Last Laugh?," 127, 128. I will push back against this latter reading at the end of the book.

98   In one of the intertitles published in the playbill (see note 22), the uniform's role in the wedding is also emphasized: "Today she cleaned her father's coat with special love; for the golden tresses were to contribute a golden radiance to the wedding celebration that evening."

99   On the importance of Jannings's body language, see Prümm, "Die bewegliche Kamera im mobilen Raum," 47. Prümm notes the camera's positioning of the porter as if "on his imaginary commanding post [*Feldherrnhügel*]."

100 The old technology of the stairwell in the tenement building of course also contrasts with the new technology of the elevator in the hotel. On the association of the stairwell with uncleanliness, see Bernard, *Lifted*, 177–80.

101 Brockmann, *A Critical History of German Film*, 82.

102 Göttler also sees a motif from the horror tradition here. On the "phantomization" of the porter, see Göttler, "Kommentierte Filmografie," 169–70.

103 Katharina Loew offers a more detailed reading of this scene, noting the complex "expressive scope" of the shots and the way the camera "realizes the shock and anguish that both characters experience." Loew, *Special Effects and German Silent Film*, 242–43.

104 For a more critical reading of the aunt's "monstrosity," see Stephan Schindler, "What Makes a Man a Man: The Construction of Masculinity in F. W. Murnau's *The Last Laugh*," *Screen* 37, no. 1 (1996): 38.

105 Dobryden, *The Hygienic Apparatus*, 121.

106 *Pace* Gehler and Kasten, who call him a "tragic hero." Gehler and Kasten, *Friedrich Wilhelm Murnau*, 74.

107 Kracauer, *From Caligari to Hitler*, 100.

108 See, e.g., Gehler and Kasten, *Friedrich Wilhelm Murnau*, 68; Tone, *Friedrich Wilhelm Murnau*, 80–81; Prümm, "Die bewegliche Kamera im mobilen Raum," 48; and Brockmann, *A Critical History of German Film*, 83. The worst offender and a cautionary example against any facile allegorizing of the film is Jean Domarchi, who emphatically declares Jannings's character an embodiment of the Wilhelmine Empire, his demotion comparable to its forced disarmament. If we are moved at all by this figure, Domarchi writes, it can only be in the way we would be by a rat run over by a car. Jean Domarchi, *Murnau* (Paris: Anthologie du cinema, 1965), 356–62.

109 Hake, "Who Gets the Last Laugh?," 127, 119.

110 Hake, "Who Gets the Last Laugh?," 119.

111 Hake, "Who Gets the Last Laugh?," 131.

112 *Pace* Silberman, *German Cinema*, 30.

113 Dobryden helpfully situates this crisis in a historical context: "The porter's failing body thus evokes a whole network of modern threats to masculinity, from women's growing social power to workplace rationalization and the trauma of war." Dobryden, *The Hygienic Apparatus*, 119.

114 On the loss of the uniform as castration, see Richard W. McCormick, *Gender and Sexuality in Weimar Modernity: Film, Literature, and "New Objectivity"* (New York: Palgrave, 2001), 27; Hake, "Who Gets the Last Laugh?," 130; and Brockmann, *A Critical History of German Film*, 84.

115 On the "feminization" of the porter, see Patrice Petro, *Joyless Streets: Women and Melodramatic Representation in Weimar Germany* (Princeton, NJ: Princeton University Press, 1989), 23–25. Petro even suggests that the feminized male might have served as a figure of identification for female audiences at the time, indeed as an alternative to a dominating patriarchy.

116 By contrast, paternal authority is precisely what is lost and then regained in the 1955 West German remake of *The Last Laugh* (dir. Harald Braun). See Ulrike Weckel,

"Reform oder Restauration väterlicher Autorität? *Der letzte Mann* (1955) als Remake mit Hans Albers," *WerkstattGeschichte* 35 (2004): 114–29.

117 On the importance of ambiguity in Murnau's work, especially in its presentation of sexuality, see Janet Bergstrom, "Sexuality at a Loss: The Films of F. W. Murnau," *Poetics Today* 6, no. 1/2 (1985): 185–203.

118 There is no consensus on how this second ending came about. Jannings claimed that he demanded it be added. Emil Jannings, *Theater–Film: Das Leben und ich* (Berchtesgaden: Verlag Zimmer & Herzog, 1951), 144. Others say Pommer intervened. Jürgen Kasten, *Carl Mayer, Filmpoet: Ein Drehbuchautor schreibt Filmgeschichte* (Berlin: Vistas Verlag, 1994), 33. If indeed the epilogue was forced upon Murnau and Mayer, then it is possible that they decided to offer up a grotesque parody of a happy ending in place of the real thing, essentially having their cake and eating it, too. Hake says it "ends up both emulating and mocking Hollywood." Hake, "Who Gets the Last Laugh?," 123.

119 Tone calls the epilogue "Brechtian"; it introduces a "shock effect" that radically breaks with the continuity of the film and thereby draws attention to its own artificiality. Tone, *Friedrich Wilhelm Murnau*, 85.

120 Gehler and Kasten also argue that the second ending "by no means contradicts or negates the fatalistic first one"; if anything, they say, it is emphasized. Gehler and Kasten, *Friedrich Wilhelm Murnau*, 75. Brockman rightly says that the epilogue in no way "eliminates the pain of the movie's real ending." Brockmann, *A Critical History of German Film*, 82.

121 The depiction of the aunt is in some ways equally as misogynistic. On this shot, see Eisner, *The Haunted Screen*, 219; Schindler, "What Makes a Man a Man," 36–38; and McCormick, *Gender and Sexuality in Weimar Modernity*, 27–28.

122 Weitz, *Weimar Germany*, 140.

123 Schechtmann, "23 December 1924," 151.

124 Kenneth S. Calhoon, *The Long Century's Long Shadow: Weimar Cinema and the Romantic Modern* (Toronto: University of Toronto Press, 2021), 94, 81. Cf. Tone, *Friedrich Wilhelm Murnau*, on the night watchman as an "angel of the night who soothes the suffering of the protagonist" (81).

125 Calhoon, *The Long Century's Long Shadow*, 79. Richard McCormick first pointed out *The Blue Angel*'s allusion to *The Last Laugh*. McCormick, *Gender and Sexuality in Weimar Modernity*, 31. Kracauer also notes the similar fates of Jannings's characters in these two films. Kracauer, *From Caligari to Hitler*, 218.

126 Elsaesser, *Weimar Cinema and After*, 44.

127 Calhoon, *The Long Century's Long Shadow*, 79. Tone says that the "spectral figure" of the night watchman makes "the truth of shadows (and thus the truth of cinema)" palpable. Tone, *Friedrich Wilhelm Murnau*, 81.

128 In a further ironic twist, the English name "Money," printed as it is in Gothic type, was misread by the creators of the English subtitles for the most recent US and UK DVD/

Blu-ray releases of the film as "Monen," obscuring what for English audiences should be an even more obvious reference.

129 Silberman, *German Cinema*, 32.

130 For Stephan Schindler, the sympathy for the porter that the film encourages only fuels a misogynistic militarism that "is not far removed from fascist mass formation." Schindler, "What Makes a Man a Man," 40.

131 Silberman, *German Cinema*, 24.

132 This language of being "locked out" (*ausgesperrt*) comes from the subsequently added intertitles, likely taken from the original screenplay. *Die Information*, xvii and playbill (see note 22).

133 Hake argues the film acknowledges the "deep contradictions" in Germany at the time in its opposing visions of modernity as either "progress and democracy" or "the worst excesses" of mechanistic modernization. Hake, "Who Gets the Last Laugh?," 125.

134 Hake, "Who Gets the Last Laugh?," 131; Elsaesser, *Weimar Cinema and After*, 247.

Printed in the United States
by Baker & Taylor Publisher Services